The best place to be?

Policy, practice and the experiences of residential school placements for disabled children

David Abbott, Jenny Morris and Linda Ward

The **Joseph Rowntree Foundation** has supported this project as part of its programme of research and innovative development projects, which it hopes will be of value to policy makers and practitioners. The facts presented and views expressed in this report are, however, those of the authors and not necessarily those of the Foundation.

Published for the Joseph Rowntree Foundation by YPS

ISBN 1 84263 051 2

© Illustrations Angela Martin 2001

Cover design by Adkins Design

Prepared and printed by:
York Publishing Services Ltd
64 Hallfield Road
Layerthorpe
York YO31 7ZQ
Tel: 01904 430033; Fax: 01904 430868; E-mail: orders@yps.ymn.co.uk

Contents

Acknowledgements

We are very grateful to the many people who took part in this research. Schools and staff facilitated our visits, local authority staff in social services and education made time for us and provided us with a rich source of qualitative and quantitative data.

We were conscious that we were asking parents about decisions that they had not taken lightly, so we are grateful for their openness with us and for taking time to be part of this project.

We wanted the experiences of disabled children and young people to be at the heart of this research report. Thank you very much to all of those we visited and spent time with.

Karen Castle, Susan Hemmings and Pippa Murray carried out some of the visits to children and young people, and the project benefited greatly from their skills.

The project also benefited from the insights and expertise of a reference group of young disabled people. Thank you to April Bird, Leon Christie, Omar Dadi, Juliet Fraser, Daniel Stivey, Helen Tilbury and Adam Walker.

We were informed and supported by a project advisory group made up of Lizzie Batten, Jane Campbell, Lesley Campbell, Karen Castle, Alia Hassan, Neil Remsbury, Philipa Russell and Peter Smith; our thanks to them for their advice.

We are grateful to the Joseph Rowntree Foundation for funding this piece of work and to Emma Stone, research manager at the Foundation, for the support she has given the project and its researchers.

Our thanks, too, to Marilyn Baker, Linda Holley and Maggi Walton at the Norah Fry Research Centre for administrative and secretarial support, and to Angela Martin for the cartoons.

1 Introduction

Despite increasing policy commitment by government to the inclusion of children with special educational needs in mainstream services, significant numbers of disabled children remain in specialist boarding schools[1] and placements continue to be made. This is an area of public policy and expenditure characterised by a lack of knowledge and understanding. We do not have a clear national picture about the numbers or needs of the children concerned; there is inadequate evidence about why such placements are made and whether they are in fact the best way to meet children's needs; and there is confusion over the implementation of local authorities' statutory duties towards them.

There is a similar dearth of qualitative research concerning disabled children's experiences at residential schools. The Hester Adrian Research Centre and Beech Tree School carried out some valuable research in the 1990s on parental views and outcomes for children with challenging behaviour and severe learning difficulties placed at the school (Robertson *et al.*, 1995, 1996). However, there has been no research on the processes by and circumstances in which disabled children come to be placed at boarding schools and none about the experiences of disabled children from their own point of view. What research there is in this field concerns either mainstream boarding schools (Morgan, 1993) or provision for children and young people with emotional and behavioural difficulties (for example, Cooper, 1992; Chaplain and Freeman, 1994; Grimshaw and Berridge, 1994; Gleeson, 1999). A literature review of education and care away from home reported:

> ... there is very little mention of disabled children within the childcare literature so that this group is in some ways 'invisible' ... this represents a significant gap in the knowledge needed to plan services appropriately. (Borland *et al.*, 1998, p. 35)

---

1 When talking about disabled children, the term 'residential school' is generally used but the term 'boarding school' is used when talking about non-disabled children. While 'residential schools' are associated with segregation and stigma, 'boarding schools' are associated with privilege and prestige. We have used both terms in this report.

This research looks at how effective current legislation and guidance is in promoting and protecting the interests of disabled children who attend residential school. We also explored:

- the circumstances in which disabled children are placed in boarding schools

- the extent to which disabled children are involved in placement decisions

- how disabled children's relationships with their families are affected by going away to school and what schools and local authorities do to nurture these relationships.

In the first stage of the project (Abbott *et al.*, 2000), the policies and practices of a representative sample of education and social services departments in 21 English authorities were examined.[2] We carried out qualitative semi-structured interviews with relevant senior managers in education and social services, and collected some statistics on disabled children and young people placed at residential schools. The main findings were as follows:

- The likelihood of a disabled child being sent to residential school varies greatly throughout the country.

- Inability to meet a child's educational needs locally and pressure on families were the two main reasons given for a disabled child going away to school.

- Whilst the joint funding of placements between education and social services departments has become more common, there were wide variations between authorities in the proportion of placements joint funded.

---

2 See the Appendix for a discussion of how the sample of 21 authorities was chosen.

- In the majority of authorities, placements funded solely by the education department attracted little or no attention from social services departments.

- There was a lack of clarity about social services departments' duties towards disabled children at boarding school.

- Education departments rarely sought the views of disabled children. Social services departments were more likely to consult with children but they did not always check to see that this was done.

- There was very little guidance for parents about the practical help they could expect in order to keep contact with their child. It was often left to the discretion of individual social workers to decide how much help to give.

The second stage of the research looked more closely at decision making and gathered information about the experiences of parents and children in four local authority areas. The four areas were selected according to a range of criteria, described in the Appendix. We did not include an authority that historically placed very low numbers of children in residential schools as we felt we would not find sufficient numbers of children and parents to interview (although we did include authorities that are currently placing very few children). With this qualification, we are confident that the issues and practices found in our case study areas will be familiar to most other local authority areas, particularly as the findings from the four areas reflect those found amongst the larger sample of 21 authorities in the first stage of the research.

Our interviews with 53 education and social services professionals, and our observations at panel meetings over a number of months in the four case study areas explored the complexities of the decision-making process. Throughout the report, we have used this interview material, and our notes from panel meetings, to illustrate the main messages that emerged from the point of view of education and social services professionals.

This second stage of the research also gathered information about the experiences of 34 parents and 32 children. The Appendix explains how the sample of parents and children was drawn. Although we have highlighted common or dominant themes that emerged in interviews with parents, children and professionals, the small numbers do not merit a quantitative analysis. The high response rate from parents (75 per cent) and children (91 per cent) means, however, we are confident that the experiences of our interviewees are broadly representative of recently made placements.

The report is structured according to the main areas of information we gathered. Chapter 2 looks at what factors parents and professionals thought led to residential school placements being made, while Chapter 3 concerns the decision-making process itself. Chapter 4 presents the experiences of disabled children and young people, including their involvement in the decision to go away to school, what it is like being at school and what it is like going home. Parents' experiences of their child's placement are covered in Chapter 5 and Chapter 6 concerns the involvement of education and social services authorities following the placement. Finally, Chapter 7 presents some key conclusions from the research along with some questions for local authorities and recommendations for government.

We have aimed to use the interview material – from professionals, parents and children – to enable the reader to gain a greater understanding of the circumstances in which disabled children are placed in boarding schools and the experiences of these placements from both the parents' and children's points of view. A parent who was a member of our Research Advisory Group, having read a draft of the report, said 'It got under my skin.' We hope that policy makers and practitioners will also find that our data gets under their skin, and thereby helps to improve the service they offer to parents and children.

2 Why are residential school placements made?

We asked parents, and social services and education professionals what factors led to residential school placements. Education and social services professionals tended to feel parents were committed, at an early stage, to the idea of a residential placement: 'I think you'll find that families that requested a residential placement, that's just what they want. They're actually fed up that you're looking at other options', said a social services team leader. In contrast, almost all the parents interviewed said that this was an option they considered reluctantly. As one parent said: 'You know I wasn't happy about residential, I didn't just arrive there, it was like a whole journey.'

While it was generally parents and sometimes professionals who initiated the possibility of a residential school, a small number of children were very positive about the idea. As we shall see when we look at their experiences in Chapter 4, this was often because of their negative experiences at local schools and their desire to have friends. Parents and professionals gave a number of reasons for boarding school placements and, while it was sometimes difficult to separate them out, we have identified three main headings: educational reasons; children's social and emotional needs; and parents' needs for support.

Educational reasons for a residential school placement

Educational issues can be divided into two main perspectives: the difficulties that local schools had in meeting children's needs; and the educational benefits that were seen to be associated with a residential setting.

Local schools

One of the main reasons for a residential placement, cited by almost all parents, was what they saw as a failure of local schools to meet their child's educational needs. Whilst they would have preferred a local option, Jane's[1] parents, for example, felt that her life chances were greater if she went out of the county:

> I wasn't going to have her somewhere out in the [local day centre] just threading beads for the rest of her life. She had worked too long and hard. She is worth more than that I'm afraid.

Education professionals were less likely to highlight inadequacies with education available locally but did acknowledge that this could sometimes be a factor. One senior educational psychologist said that, especially for children with severe learning difficulties, what 'tipped the balance' in favour of residential schools was when the local school said that they were no longer doing anything positive with the child.

---

1 We have changed the names of children to protect their identity.

Some education officers pointed out that, as more children with mild to moderate learning difficulties, and those with just a physical or a sensory impairment, are educated in mainstream schools, special schools have to cater for a wider range of needs. This poses difficulties for the schools and for some individual children. As a learning support officer said: 'Some children in the special schools have behavioural difficulties which could mean that a child with physical impairments is quite vulnerable.' This was certainly Rosalie's mother's concern about the local special school: 'She can't do anything to defend herself, she can't run, she can't call out.'

Education officers also talked of the difficulties that schools have catering for children with more complex needs: 'A child with hearing impairment and learning difficulties might have a physical impairment as well and that's where you end up thinking that you're making the best of it', said one. 'We do force compromises onto parents and sometimes I do feel that the "appropriate" is only just appropriate.'

All four of our case study areas struggled to meet the needs of children with autistic spectrum disorder in local schools. One assessment officer said: 'teachers may have limited experiences and they're not specialists in autism in the SLD schools [schools for children with severe learning disabilities]'. One of our case study areas had a specialist unit which catered for children with autism but itself had difficulty coping with the needs of some children. Two of the children in our study who had a diagnosis of autistic spectrum disorder had been offered places at local schools for children with emotional and behavioural difficulties, and their parents saw this as quite inappropriate. An assessment officer said there were some situations where a residential school placement became inevitable:

I think it's when you realise we're just containing the child. A headteacher said to me the other day: 'Yes we can cope but we're not sure if we're helping [the child].' I then say, in that situation: 'what do you need to move it from the coping to the helping?'. If they say: 'we can't do it', then we have to look at something else.

When education authorities concentrated specialist resources either within particular special schools or within designated mainstream schools, this could bring its own problems. An education officer said: 'It means some children having to travel long distances each day which, if they have high levels of physical needs, can be very difficult if not impossible for them.' The local school placement which the education authority offered to Anne would have meant her being picked up at 7.00 a.m. each morning. Her mother felt this was impossible as it took two hours every morning to get Anne ready for the day. Nick has autism and was initially attending a special school as a day pupil. However, he had a long journey to and from school and his mother thought this was hard for a six year old.

A small number of parents felt their child's physiotherapy or healthcare needs would not be met in a local school. Anne, for example, needed help with developing her balance and increasing her ability with her hands. She also needed help to prevent contractures at her knees as otherwise she would no longer be able to do standing transfers from her wheelchair, and this would have major implications for the amount of help she needed to go about her daily life. Anne's mother wanted her to go to a school which not only had specific physiotherapy sessions as part of the timetable but also could integrate her physiotherapy needs into everything else.

Rachel's mother felt that it was important that Rachel's school 'offered her everything she needed, fit management and everything under one roof which does help … and which you don't get if you go to a day school … It was the hardest decision as a parent we'll ever have to make for both me and my husband but we have to look at what we think's best for Rachel, not for us.' In Imtiaaz's case, a local school placement could not be found which would be able to cope with his tracheotomy and this was a factor in the decision to go for a residential placement.

Educational benefits of a residential setting

The educational benefits thought to be associated with a residential setting tended to be divided into two main issues: 'a 24-hour curriculum'; and the particular needs of Deaf or hearing-impaired children.

'24-hour curriculum'

There was a lack of clarity about what was meant by the phrase '24-hour curriculum', although it was used by a number of education and social services professionals, and by parents. In the first stage of this research – a survey of 21 authorities – we found that some senior education officers supported the idea of a '24-hour curriculum' while others did not (Abbott *et al.*, 2000, p. 31). In this more in-depth look at four case study areas, it became clear that *within* each authority there were varying views.

Those who did support the idea of a '24-hour curriculum' were usually referring to consistent behavioural management and to the activities that children engaged in out of school hours. Consistent behavioural management was particularly likely to be seen as important for children with autistic spectrum disorder. One assessment officer said:

Some problems are exacerbated by the fact that some home situations do not help that individual child and this is where the edge between education and social services really does blur. Sometimes you know that any good which has been done during the day will be undone totally when the child goes home at night. Not on purpose but because of limited capability of the parents. It's not because the child isn't loved; parents are trying to do their best for their child but they haven't got the right skills.

Roy's mother talked of the difficulties in coping with a child who needs constant supervision: 'It's so labour intensive mentally, not so much physically, but the endless explanation, rethinking how to get something across, how can we do this, it's so labour intensive to keep reinforcing and relearning in every situation.' Unlike many parents, however, she did think it would be possible to create consistency in managing Roy's behaviour between home and school. She felt this would require very close communication and co-operation between teachers and parents and 'no defensiveness on either part'. Moreover, she said: 'the right environment and the support services need to be in place … But because it isn't and because you see this package [a residential school] that offers all of that and you think OK this is what we'll go for.'

Patrick's mother had become convinced that a 24-hour curriculum would be the best way to support her son and for him to develop as a person. She thought it would mean a seamless crossover between being in the home setting and being at school. She thought that there would be formal lesson plans based around her son's needs and communication, and that there would be a co-ordinated approach between all staff that would run consistently between settings. The reality was in fact very different, as she explains in Chapter 5.

An education psychologist recognised that some teachers could express negative attitudes to parents who, they felt, were not following through a consistent approach at home but she thought that it was a very tall order to integrate into family life. She said she:

> ... accepted the theory of '24-hour curriculum' but I'm not sure about the practice ... In the end, I will go along with it if I can see that the whole thing is falling apart. It's the thing that parents hang their hat on. They cling to that and beat the authority over the head and that's a winning ticket.

When a need for a '24-hour curriculum' was identified it was often linked with a 52-week placement, rather than a termly placement. Most, though not all, 52-week placements involve the child coming home regularly (usually one weekend a month). Such placements were supported by professionals and parents when they felt that children responded better to short periods at home. One social worker was of the opinion, for example, that Krishnan should be in a 52-week rather than in, as he currently is, a 38-week placement. He described why:

> When he comes home, things deteriorate very quickly and that causes difficulty. This summer holiday for the first two weeks he was marvellous and then deteriorated very rapidly. He was too long at home. His parents try valiantly to deal with his presenting behaviours, but they love him to bits, and they find it very, very difficult to set the necessary boundaries.

Deaf and hearing-impaired children

Social services and education professionals held varying opinions about whether Deaf and hearing-impaired children benefit from being in a school that caters only for this group of children. Some education professionals worried about the loss of links with a local community and felt more efforts should go into finding local networks and peer groups in their local community – a task it was felt should be undertaken by social services. In one local education authority, the manager of the Deaf Services Team said: 'Residential is the last resort – because it's felt that at the end of the day the hearing impaired have to function in a hearing world and in the Deaf schools they're very much in a Deaf world.' She felt that her authority, with its specialist unit attached to a mainstream school, was able to deliver better academic standards than the Deaf schools that have traditionally been seen as offering a 'grammar school' education for Deaf children. The pressure for sending a child to such a school tended to come, she said, from Deaf parents of Deaf children who wanted their children to have access to a Deaf community and Deaf culture.

However, the viewpoint of this manager of the Deaf Services Team differed from the experience of the parent of a Deaf child who participated in the research in this local authority's area. She had initially been committed to the idea of her son going to a local school, where he should have received signing support:

> One of the teachers did pull me to one side one day and said: 'You know you really need to take a closer look at Jack, he is not happy here. And more to the point he is not learning anything. He is the one at the back of the class chewing the pencil because I can't sign for him.'

In another local education authority, the Manager of the Sensory Impairment Team was of the firm opinion that children whose first language was British Sign Language (BSL) should be educated in a signing environment from as early an age as possible and that this could not be achieved within local schools:

I think that we've always considered that out-of-county schools are a continuum of the provision we've made locally … The Team are very committed to support children in local schools but we do see the need for peer groups – communication peer groups – and meeting children's needs to be independent learners … I would say that a child needs to be included within an education environment both academically and socially in order that the child can succeed in both of those areas. What we're aiming for eventually is that the child becomes a citizen who will be able to be part of the local community but there may be different ways of getting there and it may not be through inclusion in a mainstream class where the child can be excluded academically and socially.

He did, however, feel that sometimes parents' wish for a residential placement was not so much about recognising the need for a signing environment but that:

… they are really rejecting a comprehensive education for their children rather than mainstream education per se. [The school they want their child to go to] has a reputation for providing a 'grammar school' kind of education, has small classes and so on.

It is very difficult in reality to separate educational and social needs. From a child's point of view, if their social experience – their interaction with their peers – is negative, this will have an impact on how they feel about school and on their learning potential. This is explored in the next section when we look at how children's social and emotional needs figured in the pressures for boarding school placements.

Children's social and emotional needs

Both parents and professionals identified the social and emotional consequences for children of the difficulties that local schools sometimes have in meeting children's needs. A small number of children themselves also told us about their difficult experiences of local schools and how this led them to feel that a boarding school would be better.

Peer groups

A child or young person who spends their school life in a situation where they have little or no contact with anyone else who shares the same experiences can feel very isolated.

Sometimes, the effects of impairment itself can create a distance from non-disabled peers. The manager of a Visual Impairment Team in one education authority described one girl's difficulties in interacting with her peers and her resulting isolation:

> I think some of her difficulties were because she missed the visual expressions and body language of people because of her visual impairment and that made it difficult to fine-tune her communication.

In this kind of situation, this Visual Impairment Team will usually try to support the child to overcome barriers to making friends and will also try to bring together young people with similar experiences from across the area. However, this Team has limited resources for this kind of activity and the need for a peer group was one reason why the Team Manager supported some young people with visual impairments going to residential colleges following GCSEs:

I really believe in inclusion but I think we also need to think about what do they get when they're not in inclusive education because there are some benefits like having a peer group that is visually impaired and not thinking they're the only one in the whole wide world that's got this disability.

There can be similar isolation experienced by Deaf and hearing-impaired children. In one authority, a specialist unit attached to a mainstream secondary school was said to deliver a good standard of education but had only 15 children. A girl who joined the unit had no one in her year group who was Deaf or hearing impaired. In another area, a parent of a Deaf child felt that the social and emotional problems her daughter was experiencing were almost wholly connected with her isolation and lack of friends at her local mainstream school. There were no other Deaf children of her daughter's age in her year group and outside of school her Deaf friends were older than her: 'She was a very bubbly girl but became very isolated. She … had no friends. Not at home nor at school really.' Like most of the parents in our study, this mother was reluctant to consider residential school but became increasingly concerned that her daughter was doing badly by not going away.

As children with a diagnosis of autistic spectrum disorder get older, the consequences of their impairment can mean that they do not develop the friendships and social activities that non-disabled children have outside school hours. As David's mother said: 'When he came home from school at 3.30 his life was ended, he had nothing.' When she went to look at residential schools, the thing that most impressed her was, as she put it: 'the social side of it … you know, they finish their school day and they're doing things, they're learning guitar, they go for trips at the weekend, they're always doing something … and I thought he would make friends.'

If a child has to travel a long way to a day school, they may not have friends to play with after school. Jack's mother said:

My other boys are able to walk down the road and knock on their friends' house and their friends come back and they have had friends stay over. Jack had no one. Jack had no house he could walk to.

Sometimes, however, it is the attitudes of non-disabled peers that create isolation. One social worker described how a child with significant physical impairments was included in her peer group at a mainstream school up until the age of about 12: 'but, after that, the other children went their own ways and she fell behind socially as well as academically'. Her social worker concluded:

There wasn't any peer group for her, she had to go away in order to get her own identity, to get away from having to fit in with other people ... And that led to a placement which has been very successful ... she's blossomed, she's matured ... It has certainly changed my view about whether some residential placements are the right thing.

Anne's mother said that Anne's lack of friends when she was at a mainstream primary school was one reason she wanted her to go to a special school where she thought she would have more chance of making friends:

Towards the end of her time at primary school, she was extremely unhappy and at times it was quite difficult to make her go to school.

Children's experiences of local education

There are some situations where the 'presenting problem' is the difficulties that parents are having in coping with their child's behaviour at home where, nevertheless, parents feel that the real cause of the difficulties is to be found in the child's experiences at school. Krishnan's parents, for example, were committed to their son being included in his local school and only reluctantly came to the conclusion, as he progressed through his secondary education, that this was not working for him. Krishnan has Asperger's Syndrome and his parents found that he needs a very structured situation and a lot of help to maximise his learning potential. He wasn't getting this at school, he found homework very difficult, he was being bullied and his self-esteem was very low. His parents felt that it was his anxiety about all of this that resulted in obsessive behaviours at home of a kind which made life very difficult, particularly because he was getting more violent as he got older and experienced more pressure at school.

Ryan also had Asperger's Syndrome and his mother described his time in mainstream middle school as 'the worst time of our lives':

> We had all these incidents – his shoes going out the window, he was beat up on the bus, his bag was stolen. It was just one thing after the other and the school were constantly phoning telling me how awful he was and the teacher he had didn't like him at all. As a punishment, she would refuse to let him look at the computer or use the computer even though that was one of his passions.

One parent's application for a residential placement was supported by a health professional who wrote: 'The anxiety he experiences on going to school appears to exacerbate his difficulties and his presenting symptoms.' The 'presenting symptoms' included self-harm as well as violent behaviour towards his brother. A number of parents, and a few professionals, spoke of children experiencing significant emotional distress as a result of their experience of local schooling.

Encouraging independence

Some young disabled people want to go away to residential school or college in order to experience more independence. Sometimes, social services or education professionals feel that young people would benefit from specialist input and/or experience that would enable them to be more independent. A visually impaired child may need assistance to enable them to learn to do all the things that non-disabled children learn routinely as they grow into adolescence: use roads and transport independently, make a cup of tea or sandwiches for their lunch, cook their own supper, and so on. However, they may not receive this assistance. In one authority, the Visual Impairment Team identified this need but said they could not provide it because their role was limited to enabling children to access the curriculum; specialist social workers were supposed to offer some assistance but were generally too over-stretched to do much. If parents were not able to encourage such independence, this could have a very significant impact on young people's social experiences.

A few education and social services professionals felt that a young person would benefit from going away to school or college, particularly if there was a concern that parents were 'over-protective' or had low expectations of their child's ability to be independent.

Child protection issues

We were told of situations where concern about a child's welfare resulted in a residential school placement. This was seen as a way of ensuring that the child received a better standard of care, which could also mean they were better able to achieve their educational potential. One social worker felt that sometimes the demands of looking after a disabled child may so undermine a family's ability to cope that this can have a detrimental affect on the welfare of the child:

> The family unit is in crisis and the whole focus is on the disabled child … So we have to draw back and think about what the child's needs are … So you start hedging towards a child protection situation where you're looking at protecting the interests of the child.

Sometimes, however, a boarding school placement was made because no other placement was available when a child had to be removed from their home. One such situation involved 15-year-old Maeve, about whom the Disability Team had been concerned for some time. An incident resulted in an emergency referral to the Children and Families Team and removal from her home. However, the Children and Families Team could not find a suitable placement for her, as the social worker from the Disability Team explained:

> We were sent to look at the children's homes in the borough and none of them were suitable for a child in a wheelchair and even the children weren't suitable for her to be with really. I was racing all over [the authority and neighbouring areas], looking at proposed placements which were no good at all. And then the worker from Children and Families said to me: 'well, what about her going to [residential school]?' and I thought well it's a good idea because she's not doing very well at school, she's not getting any help at home with her homework … She'd lapsed behind so much because she's been so unhappy for such a while.

Family support issues

The majority of parents in this study spoke of not getting the support they needed if their child was to remain at home. Rosalie's parents asked for help with adapting their home, to make it easier to look after their daughter who has high personal assistance needs, but it took years to get the adaptations needed, by which time Rosalie had gone to boarding school. It was more common, however, for parents to be seeking support in coping with their child's behaviour and they were often critical of the attitudes of social workers, and the amount and type of support available. Ryan's mother, for example, described a social worker's reaction to her request for help:

> Between the smashing the car and the smashing the kitchen incident a man from social services came to see us. He sat on the settee and said to me, 'There's nothing wrong with Ryan. He's a real rager. He just has a temper and we have to try and curb it.' He wasn't in the business to take children away, he said. We weren't asking him to take him away, we just wanted help. We couldn't believe what he was saying.

Roy's mother explained the difficulties she and her family experienced. She said that Roy, aged eight and with a diagnosis of autistic spectrum disorder, 'controlled our conversation, our breathing, our eating, you couldn't have any personality, you had to keep your voice at a monotone, or he became really uptight'. She was particularly worried about her daughter who, aged ten was, she said:

… losing out … being in the same school she would be told, 'oh your brother is spastic, your brother is gay' – because he used to kiss other people inappropriately – and so they'd go, 'your brother is mental, don't play with them it might be catching' … She was quite sensitive about it because she didn't have any freedom at home and was beginning to feel that there was no freedom at school. She gave up everything she did and … wanted to kill herself … It sounds terribly pathetic but we had become totally housebound and I just longed to do something with my daughter like walk up the street and go to the post office … I asked at the hospital, the clinic, child management, everywhere, tell us some technique for managing this child … We sought help from everywhere we could, nothing.

Patrick's mother also felt that things had become overwhelmingly difficult for her at home but found, like the majority of parents interviewed, that access to respite was limited. Nevertheless, in common with a number of other parents, she felt guilty about asking for any more. Ben's parents talked of how 'lucky' and 'grateful' they were to have a respite service one night a week, although they also said it was not nearly enough.

Patrick and Ben's parents were amongst a small minority of parents in our study who were happy with the local schools, but who talked of how their need for more support affected them and their child, and led them to conclude a residential school was in their child's best interests. Ben's parents said:

The schooling was fine, it's just too difficult to cope … it was beginning to break down … We just felt we had to be almost cruel to be kind, that he was not going to progress as a human being unless he went away.

The information gathered from local authorities confirmed that there was often limited support available if a child remained living at home. For example, we observed at social services resources panels where sometimes it was possible to see, in a situation under discussion, that a lack of support at an early age might well lead – in a few years' time – to pressure from parents for residential education. Some workers felt that lack of support meant it was almost inevitable that some children would be placed in residential schools, and some also identified the need for early intervention to prevent this happening. One social work team leader said:

> I think a lot of problems could be solved early on if there were adequate behavioural input early on. There's virtually no psychology and no psychiatric input into disabled kids at all here. You end up in situations where you know things are going to get worse and worse, and you're looking at a kid who, in the end, there's going to be family breakdown and moving into some really, really expensive placement for lack of resources and co-ordination of resources early on.

Even when social services managers had recognised a need for greater support, it was often not possible to provide this, particularly for children with a diagnosis of autistic spectrum disorder or severe learning disabilities. As one commissioning officer said: 'We just don't have the specialist services and, even if we tried to develop them, I'm not sure we could recruit the staff … we have enough difficulty recruiting care workers as it is.' In one case study area, we were told of how, in order to cater for one child who was violent and harmed himself, the residential respite unit had to be closed to other users.

Shared (respite) care with link families was generally not available for parents with autistic children. Local authorities had been unable to find suitable families and, where they had, the relationships often broke down quickly. Kate's mother said:

> They wanted us to try a respite family but they couldn't find a family that would take her. By the time she was six, we had been through four families and the last family had her for about an hour-and-a-half and they brought her back and said, 'sorry we can't cope'.

Social workers and their managers told us of the difficulties they had in supporting some families. One social services team leader thought that better financed packages of support would help some families but that a minority of children required such high levels of care it would be difficult to ever provide this:

> I think there are some children … who really need a very high level of supervision who we'd really struggle with … For a lot of children, residential school is the only option to meet their care needs.

Another social worker felt that, while good packages of support could be put together to prevent a residential school placement, such support could be fragile in the face of all the changes that take place within families and high staff turnover:

> It's the stress of trying to find a package, so part of you feels that you should make every effort and the other part of you thinks, 'Oh God, will I ever do it?'

A local package of support is not always cheaper than a residential school placement. One of our case study areas was faced with having to find alternative provision for five children whose residential school was being closed down. The senior manager calculated that the amount currently being spent on the five placements would not fund the level of 24-hour support that the children needed if they were to be brought back into the area: 'The economics of it just don't stack up.'

A few professionals interviewed felt that sometimes a parent's request for a residential school was motivated by a rejection of their disabled child and that boarding school was a more socially acceptable option than placing a child in care. As one social worker said: 'It's quite sad that they were thinking of sending their child away when he was four. I think it's [so] that his family don't end up with impaired children.' In a small number of cases amongst the parents we interviewed, social workers had suggested an alternative family or formal care as an alternative to boarding school. The parents concerned had resisted this, saying they did not want to give up their parenting role to anyone else. One parent also said the suggestion implied that she had totally failed as a parent and that somebody else would not fail.

Karen's mother's experience had been of too many professionals being involved in her daughter's life and feeling that her home was constantly invaded. Some social workers were similarly of the opinion that a package of effective support could mean a lot of people going into the home, which some families could not accept. On the other hand, there were some parents who *did* want support provided in their own home but social services were unable to offer this.

The financial and practical barriers to providing the levels of support needed to some families sat uneasily alongside some professionals' outright opposition to residential school placements. One senior social services manager stated: 'From a personal point of view, I resist residential schools as much as I can because it doesn't sit comfortably with me, you know, children being sort of "shipped away" and sort of forgotten about really.' At the same time, she admitted that 'the most we can really offer families is a weekend a month plus a bit of outreach support and sometimes that's not enough.'

Conclusions

While the professionals interviewed for this study often tried to separate out 'social' and 'educational' factors in terms of whether a residential placement was felt to be necessary, parents tended to see a closer connection between the two aspects of their children's lives and needs. A few parents told us of teachers and social workers who seemed to understand their child's needs and the impact on their families' lives. The majority, however, spoke of a lack of understanding and inadequate support at school and at home, leading to their conclusion that a specialist residential setting was the only way of meeting their child's needs and those of their family. As we shall see, the decision-making process that led to a boarding school placement was usually characterised by conflict between parent and authority, and often conflict between the education and social services authority.

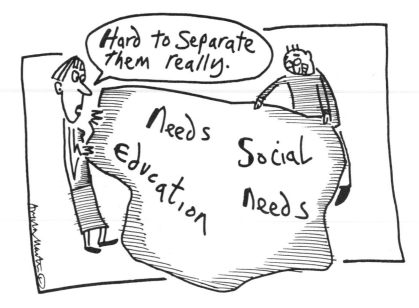

3 The process of decision making by local authorities

In our interviews with 34 parents, we explored their experiences of the decision-making process that led to a residential school placement. We also interviewed a total of 53 senior managers and front-line workers from the education and social services departments of our case study areas about their perspectives. In each case study area, we observed at meetings of the panels that took decisions about these placements.

Parents' experiences

Only one parent spoke positively about the decision-making process. This was Rachel's mother: 'I must say they were brilliant, they are a quite good authority, we're very lucky.' However, the placement was made in 1992, when Rachel was four-and-a-half, and was characterised by some lack of interest on the part of the education authority. She had been going to a nursery specialising in conductive education and the staff recommended a boarding school. The local education authority agreed, apparently with no hesitation, to fund the placement. They rarely come to annual reviews of her Statement of special educational needs.

A change in attitudes towards residential school placements in this and other authorities means that usually parents no longer find the decision-making process easy. In only one of our four case study areas was getting agreement to such a placement relatively straightforward. In the other three authorities, it could sometimes take years to get a placement agreed, often after a tribunal or the threat of one.

Almost all of the parents interviewed felt they had to fight the local authority, although, in one area, the disagreements tended to come at the stage of choosing a school rather than in the initial decision to make a residential placement. Many felt the process was designed to be difficult:

> I think they make it so hard higher up with all these letters and all these bits of paper and everything else and these sort of damning reports that lots of people back down.

Some saw it in quite personal terms such was the detrimental impact it had on their lives:

> I know they have a duty to spend money in the most cost-effective way but, my God, how many times can you kick someone knowing that I am the one looking after a really needy little boy ... I really felt thoroughly persecuted.

A number of parents spoke of individual teachers saying they could not meet a child's needs but the school and the education authority saying they could. Even when the school formally supported a residential placement, the education authority might still oppose it. This was Krishnan's parents' experience: a three year fight for an alternative placement ended only when the local school excluded him.

Parents also often found it difficult to get social services professionals to focus on the needs of their child, in the face of a general opposition to boarding school placements. One parent recounted:

> I had a social worker and her senior manager sitting in my living room saying: 'We don't believe in residential schools' and I said: 'Can we talk about my child's needs?'

Other parents faced what they thought were prejudicial and hurtful attitudes towards them and an assumption that they didn't want their children any more:

> They said the only reason we wanted her to go away was because we wanted her out of the way.

In one of our case study areas, the senior social services manager talked of 'designing a system which had the intention of limiting access to this kind of placement, not just for financial reasons but because we know that some of the establishments were not satisfactory and it was difficult to maintain sufficient contact.' A parent in this area who was requesting social services support for a boarding school placement would be told (to quote a letter received by one of the parents in our sample):

> Social services funding for out of county placements is restricted to children and young people whose situation requires them to be looked after by the local authority and for whom there is no appropriate foster home or residential placement in county. I do not know whether this applies to [your daughter] but I will talk to [the manager at the respite centre] and if you wish ask a social worker to visit to make a formal assessment of [your daughter's] needs and home circumstances.

The parent who received this letter said that she took this to mean that 'if you're no longer able to look after Anne – if you want her to go into care – we'll come and do an assessment.' This parent did not realise that her daughter already had 'looked after' status under Children Act regulations as she used an overnight short-break service.

The senior manager explained:

> We found it quite helpful to adopt that position ... We had some substantial stand-offs with parents who very explicitly wanted boarding schools for their children. And we found it quite helpful to say: 'well you realise this means your child will be looked after and allocated a social worker.'

In this particular case, as in a number of others, the parent concerned then appealed to the Special Educational Needs (SEN) Tribunal. Once she had won her case, the local education authority paid the full costs of the placement with no contribution, or involvement, of social services.

A social worker in a different authority adopted a similar approach:

> Parents quite often like the idea of residential school because it is easier than saying 'My child's in care', so, in some ways, it's quite nice to be able to point out, 'Well you can pretend your child's in residential school, but actually she's still looked after legally.'

Ben's father was told social services would look for a foster family for Ben: 'We said, absolutely no way. But they still went ahead and advertised.' Parents felt that being told that social services were going to have to look for an 'alternative family' was a way of putting pressure on them to reconsider.

In contrast, some parents felt forced to say that they could no longer look after their child. Kate's mother was told, by her social worker, that she would have to say she couldn't cope if she wanted to get the placement funded. Robert's mother, having been through months when education and social services delayed making a decision, finally asked the social services department to place him with a foster carer. She said, 'Because I work within the system I knew they wouldn't find one … It was horrible.' David's mother went down to the Civic Centre one evening: 'I said, take him into care … I can't cope any more.'

Very few parents were clear about who took the decision on whether their child could go to a boarding school. Their experience was more commonly of a long drawn-out process, with sometimes information being conveyed about how 'it has to go to panel', but not knowing who was on the panel, when it met, why it made the decisions it did. Patrick's mother spoke of 'faceless, nameless people that I never even got to know who they were. I wasn't even allowed to know.'

It was not unusual for the decision-making process to take more than a year. Patrick's mother explained her experience:

> In February 1998, they had said it should take about six months. I thought Patrick would be at a residential school in September 1998. And then I thought January 1999. And then I thought September 1999. And then I thought January 2000 and it went on and on. I actually thought Easter 2000 … In the end, it was September 2000. It was like living completely in limbo. It was just terrible.

It was also very common for parents to lack information about what was happening within the decision-making process. Rosalie's mother was told in the January of her daughter's last year at primary school that 'It's going to panel':

> I didn't know what panel. I kept being told: 'The panel hasn't sat yet' and I would ask 'Well when are they sitting?' and they would say 'The date has not been set' … They were waiting for different statements to come in. A statement from the pediatric consultant, all these people had to write their bit. That all started in January and then in July we were still waiting.

How we make decisions — Well usually on a Thursday, but it's a secret recipe.

Decision Making Process……

In the event, Rosalie's mother was never told the panel's decision and the first she knew about it was when the authority's transport service rang to arrange to pick Rosalie up and take her to school at the beginning of the September term. Four years after first applying, Kate's parents were never officially told in writing that their application had been agreed. Neeta's mother turned up for her tribunal only to be told that her authority had written to the tribunal two days before to say they were going to fund the placement. No one from the authority had let her know.

Neeta's mother felt that conflicting advice about the best education for her daughter, who has a hearing impairment, contributed to Neeta's emotional difficulties. It took a year and a half to agree the placement:

> I felt that she wasn't mine any more, that I didn't have any say or couldn't make any decision over what I wanted for her. It's not very nice when somebody else takes over your child really.

A few parents decided that it was important to appear to be doing the 'right thing', whether this was visiting local schools they were asked to look at, allowing their child to be considered for an alternative family, or adopting conciliatory tones with professionals. Ben's father said:

> We played the game as such and we did everything we were told. You need to go along with them and, if they tell you to look at schools, you must go and look at them. You have to do everything that they ask you to do. MENCAP [Royal Society for Mentally Handicapped Children and Adults] told us not to involve solicitors and I think that was an excellent piece of advice because, as soon as I said I wasn't going to do that, there was a definite sea change in attitude.

However, other parents had employed solicitors to work on their behalf and some parents had advocates to help them. It was not unusual for parents to have written to their MPs or councillors for support. Those who did found that it brought faster and more favourable responses from their local authority. Karen's mother had applied for a placement that required tripartite funding. Each department had been arguing about the level of funding they were prepared to commit. Karen wrote to her MP and a couple of weeks later it was all agreed.

Local authorities' perspectives on the decision-making process

Within our four case study areas, there was a general wish to avoid residential school placements, although some individual officers were in favour of them. As one senior learning support officer said: 'As far as I'm concerned, every child has an entitlement to go to their local school if at all possible.' And an education psychology manager said: 'We place a high value on inclusion ... It's hard to see where residential education fits into a social inclusion agenda.'

Another senior learning support officer talked of the wider implications of each boarding school placement: 'You only have to make one residential placement and you've got the cost of one full-time teacher – and then you have difficulty finding the money for supporting local provision.' A senior education officer pointed out:

Our duty is to meet needs and not to make ideal provision. There is a tension between our aim to meet the needs of all children in [the area] and parents who want the best for their child.

One parent partnership worker reflected:

The education department has done an about turn on inclusion in recent years … They used to say, 'Well, if the child needs that much support, they ought to be in a special school.'… [Now] they say, 'If we can support this child in a mainstream school, we will do it' … I think the culture is that they want as much money as possible of the special needs budget to go into supporting children in mainstream schools and that the only way they can free up money is to reduce the number of out-of-county placements.

Nevertheless, a principled opposition to residential placements could sometimes be undermined by involvement with individual children. An assessment officer said:

I personally hate anything to do with residential schooling … But I think in some children's cases they do get more out of that environment than they do in their home environment … they do get a more consistent approach and they also don't get the impact of a very long day because of the long journey to and from school every day.

One social services team leader felt that arguments about inclusion could go on for so long that, in the end, the needs of the child were lost sight of. The kind of practical barriers referred to in the last chapter (such as difficulties in providing specialist support to meet the needs of small numbers of children) were sometimes felt to be in conflict with the principle of inclusion. An educational psychologist said: 'I have to balance the general support towards the moral agenda of inclusion versus low incidence and complex needs.' It could also be felt that inclusion policies perhaps do not encompass all disabled children. As one educational psychologist said: 'You have to recognise that the Government does endorse segregation for children like these.'

Front-line workers talked about difficulties in their relationships with parents who wanted a boarding school placement. Some educational psychologists (EPs) spoke of being caught between colleagues opposed to residential schools and families who wanted the best for their child. A number regretted the limitations of their role:

> EPs should have ... more time to spend with families talking to them about what it will mean, rather than what seems to happen where you write some kind of advice and then you're divorced from the rest of the process. Ideally, an EP should have some co-ordinating role or contact lead role with the family.

Social workers also felt that they did not have enough time to support a family through the decision-making process. They often felt like natural advocates for a family but occupied a difficult position when the authority's decision was contested.

Concerns about a case possibly going to tribunal had an impact on how authorities wanted professionals to relate to parents, and also on recommendations to panel meetings. One parent partnership worker confirmed that schools sometimes felt inhibited from saying there were educational reasons for an out-of-county placement:

> I think if they speak out they're reprimanded ... I've heard it ... they're very loath to say so because they know the education department doesn't want to fund out-of-county placements.

Whilst the policy was that individual workers should not name specific schools in reports they wrote, parents often told us that individual workers told them 'privately' that they supported a particular school. A senior educational psychologist confirmed that this happened, but spoke of not wishing to tie the hands of budget-holders or to harm the authority's case at tribunal: 'in terms of professionalism, I wonder about psychologists … saying things privately to parents, but yes it's real.'

Front-line workers, whether in education or social services departments, often felt as removed from the decision-making process as parents did. The Manager of one education authority's Deaf Services Team said:

> My service has no say, we write the reports but it's the panel that makes the decision and often they don't know the children.

Some workers were also critical of the way parents were treated. A social work team leader said:

> The whole process of the panel works best for the department; it does not help the parents. And to not give clear decisions to parents straightaway is the worst thing the panel could ever do. They take no responsibility for the fact that they sit there and they make the decisions and parents want to know. I've got a two-line memo saying 'no, no', and then I'm supposed to phone the parents and tell them.

The placement panels

All our case study areas reported an increase in collaboration between education and social services over recent years. The main mechanisms for this co-operation were the panels which met monthly. In one area, this was a joint panel with social services and education; the other three included health too. In each area, the panel was chaired by a senior education officer.

Only one of the case study areas had a pooled budget. This meant that if either department made a decision that a residential school placement should be made, then the funding would be met out of the pooled budget. Such decisions were reported to the panel for formal agreement, but also to check that all local solutions had been exhausted before the placement was agreed.

In each of the case study areas, a lot of decisions had already been taken before a particular case was taken to the panel. As one senior education officer said: 'The panel is the end of a very long line of decision making.' Both education and social services had usually considered a need for additional support at their own learning support (education) and resources (social services) panels. Some children had been discussed a number of times at one or both of these types of panel.

When a case got to panel, there was often disagreement about whether it was a failure of social services or education to meet the child's needs which might make a residential placement necessary. In a number of these cases, the issue was not resolved at the panel meeting and the decision about a placement was put off for further investigation.

The following notes, taken from observation at a series of panel meetings in one authority, are one example of how decisions were delayed by conflict between education and social services.

Child Y, aged eight, with physical impairments, was being looked after by elderly grandparents who were repeatedly threatening to 'dump' her at the doorstep of a children's hospital because they couldn't cope. Education want her to go to a local special school but social services say this won't make a difference. The request for joint funding from social services for a residential school placement goes on for a number of months. Education continue to resist on the grounds that they can meet her educational needs locally. The relationship between social services and education is getting 'strained'. After a panel meeting the senior education and social services managers discuss the issue privately. The education chair has been asked by his boss to ask 'some direct questions' of social services, such as, 'are there no family link schemes, no other local resource?' Social services say the options have all been exhausted. The only alternative is a private agency placement which can be £700–800 a week. Education is anxious that they are being perceived by the family as 'villains'. Meanwhile the family has got the support of the local MP and the education chair acknowledges that with it they would probably end up losing at a tribunal and have to pay the whole bill. He lets social services know that their request for joint funding will be agreed.

Apart from arguments over responsibilities, there were a number of other factors that made it difficult for panels to effectively focus on the needs of individual children. Perhaps most crucially, they were usually hampered by the absence of anyone at the meeting who had met the child or family. For example, in the case of one child, the school, the educational psychologist and the social worker had agreed that a boarding school placement was the best option. However, when the papers went to panel, the decision was queried on the grounds that members of the panel were not sure that all local options had been explored. The social worker who had written the report had not realised how much emphasis she needed to put on all the work that had been done before coming to the recommendation and, because no one at the panel knew the child, the decision was delayed for two months (the panel did not meet over the summer), which meant the child could not start at the beginning of the autumn term.

It can be very different when someone is present at the panel meeting who does know the child or has had direct contact with the parent. One panel discussion was observed where the chair of the panel had been contacted by the child's mother, which led to a more detailed knowledge of the situation and some sympathy for the mother's case. Opposition was expressed by another panel member (who had not been in direct contact with the child or mother), arguing that the current mainstream school placement should be appropriate if the right support was put in. The panel chair, however, argued that 'we shouldn't punish a child for a weakness in our system … we haven't met his needs so far and it's unfair that he should suffer any longer because of this.'

There were times when panels had incomplete written assessments on which to base their decisions and one panel meeting was observed where there was no written information at all about any of the children discussed at the meeting. When a comprehensive assessment *was* part of the information available, it could make a real difference to the understanding of the child's needs (as long as the panel members had read the papers, or someone took responsibility for presenting the information). One discussion, for example, was transformed from a disagreement about whether social services could respond to a parent's request for support, to a more holistic consideration of the child's needs, by the presentation of a written report from an interdisciplinary health team. This highlighted the impact of the child's unhappiness at school on his behaviour at home, making clear that – from the child's perspective at least – his needs could not be neatly divided amongst different service responsibilities. The assessment highlighted how his educational and social needs were not being met at school, how this increased his anxiety levels and the implications this had for his behaviour at home. Without this clear link being made, the tendency had been for the problem to be identified as his mother's inability to cope with his behaviour and social services' inability to respond to her requests for respite.

Sometimes, the needs of children with emotional and behavioural difficulties dominated panel meetings with little time to discuss the needs of disabled children in any detail. Expertise on the needs of disabled children was sparsely represented on some panels. Panel meetings routinely took over two hours and, in two areas, sometimes as many as 25 children were discussed (in the other two areas, it was more common for about five or six children to be discussed, although the meetings could also take up to two hours). In these situations, children discussed towards the end of the meeting tended to receive less attention than those nearer the beginning. At some panels, there was a lot of paperwork and not all of it was read. A social work team leader said: 'You're lucky if you've had a chance to glance properly at the reports at all.' The following extract from notes taken from observation at one panel is a fairly typical example of this particular panel's deliberations:

> The panel receives a report recommending that a girl, with physical and hearing impairments in Year 9, should move from a mainstream school to a special residential school. Social services representative wonders if a school for the Deaf has any places. By now all the EBD [emotional and behavioural difficulties] representatives have put their papers away. The one other MLD [moderate learning disabilities]/SLD representative isn't interested because she's too able for his school. The Chair leafs through the papers reading bits out aloud as he comes across them. No one seems to have a clear picture of the child's needs. Social services representative then says making progress on communication is vital. Chair agrees but says there is no report from the hearing impaired service. He reads on and then finds a report from the hearing impaired service saying she should go to an MLD school. Eventually, the Chair decides to reject area panel's recommendation and to check if there are places at a school for the Deaf.

As we found in the first stage of the research, the role of health authorities was under-developed. One panel member from education said: 'really we haven't got health on board. It's like they live upstairs and we live downstairs.' In one case study area, the health representatives did not have the power to make financial decisions on behalf of the authority and were uncertain about how to arrange a health contribution.

In contrast, in another authority, health and social services had worked together to produce a continuing care policy specifically for children. This meant that, although the health authority was not represented on the panel, the senior social services manager could 'go to health and say this child comes within the policy, we then agree that health contribute and all the procedures are in place to do this'. However, this arrangement seemed to break down when the senior social services manager left.

It was easy to see, from observation of panel meetings, how the delays that parents complained of came about. Decisions were deferred when a particular panel member was absent, when a panel had not received the paperwork it required, when there was disagreement about the information they had been given, or when they did not know whether a particular school would take a child.

Choosing a school

By the time an application 'got to panel', the parent had usually identified a boarding school but was unlikely to have received any assistance from education or social services in doing this. In one of the case study areas, a social worker with a number of children with autism on his caseload had built up knowledge of some residential schools and advised parents on which to look at. One parent was helped by the headteacher of her daughter's local school, who had even visited a school with her. This level of assistance, however, seemed unusual and the majority of parents said they received little help in choosing a school.

Some social workers recognised this as a problem. One social worker for Deaf children recounted how:

> … parents look to us for advice and then we in turn get our knuckles rapped by the education department because they would say to us 'You can't recommend to parents what school their children should go to' … There is a big gap, there needs to be people offering parents support, where to go and how to do it.

In another authority, the social work team leader said it was unclear whose responsibility it was to look at schools:

> [Education] seem to have a list of schools … Then it often seems to be left to parents to go and have a look. I think it's right that parents should be involved in that decision and for us to look at social and care needs but education should also be involved especially where the child's needs might be quite complex … I wish they had someone whose job it was to do that.

There was little evidence of any real assessment by education or social services professionals about whether a school was likely to meet a child's care needs. Education authorities did not consider this to be their role when making placements: 'We would focus on education rather than on care. If social services were joint funding, they may be involved in looking at the school', said one senior education officer. In this authority, the majority of out-of-authority placements were still funded solely by education so there would be no social services involvement in most cases. The education officer went on to say:

> There's an assumption that, because we use the same schools again and again, we would know if there were any problems. Also it's down to the parents, we assume parents would be looking at the care side of it.

Even when there was social services involvement, there did not seem to be much attention paid to assessing the standard of care provided by a school, prior to a placement being made. We were sometimes told an authority had a checklist to evaluate a school when a placement was being considered, but no one could produce an example. In one authority, a social services manager told us there was a list of written criteria but she was not able to provide us with a copy, and when a social worker, who had been involved in the placement of five children, was asked about this list, he replied: 'Well I've never seen it.' Another senior manager said: 'We used to have a checklist years and years ago but I think that's gone by the board.'

Inspection reports on schools were not often referred to. In one authority, a social services manager said that they did not look at inspection reports 'because we don't see them as looked after children' (in other words, residential school placements were not seen as being covered by Children Act regulations). The same authority had recently discovered that one school where they placed a number of children 'had not been inspected by the local social services Inspection Unit at all. We only discovered [this] when we contacted them after there was an allegation about a child who was coming home with marks on his back.'

While each authority had formal decision-making procedures for agreeing placements, this tended to focus on whether an out-of-authority placement was necessary, not on whether a particular placement was suitable. As one senior manager said: 'the report which goes to panel doesn't deal with the school, it deals with why the placement is needed.' When social services and education did get involved in finding a placement, it was often not a case of choosing a school but finding one that could take the child concerned.

In contrast, almost all the parents interviewed put considerable effort into finding a school they felt would be right for their child. As Roy's mother explained:

> I made a career of it. I just wrote to every school I could think of, searching through the books, any school that I thought might be a possibility … I wrote to everywhere from Derby down to the Isle of Wight … I did a year's visiting, anywhere I thought was within reasonable travelling distance.

Sara's mother had a mental checklist of what she was looking out for, including the physical environment, the attitudes and approach of staff, and access to specialist facilities like physiotherapy. Many parents said the things they looked for most were whether the school was open, welcoming and flexible about their child coming home, and whether parents could visit.

Other parents were often a more important source of information than social services or education professionals. Some voluntary organisations helped and sometimes it was pure chance that a parent found a school they liked: 'It was pure fluke. I knew somebody who was on the board of governors there … no one made it easy for me to find out because ultimately they don't want the children out of county.' Parents were, on the whole, surprised at how little help they got in thinking about which schools might be appropriate.

It is not that parents don't want help in assessing schools. As Rosalie's mother said: 'I wanted … someone in authority to visit the schools to ask the questions that I felt unable to ask … I wanted the reassurance.' Patrick's mother wanted a partnership approach rather than feeling that the onus was on her to find a school: 'Ideally there would have been somebody co-ordinating. Ideally I would have been working hand in hand with the LEA [local education authority] looking at schools.'

Parent partnership workers did not seem to play a significant role in assisting parents who were thinking about residential school. None of the parents interviewed had had any contact with a parent partnership worker. In one authority, the parent partnership worker said she would try and put a parent in touch with another parent who shared similar experiences, while, in another authority, the worker said: 'I'd be very loath to enter into a discussion with a parent about residential schools.'

Conclusions

Parents generally had little information about the decision-making process. They spoke of long delays and of being forced into conflict with their local authority. They wanted more help with choosing a school but were unlikely to receive this. They often felt that general policies were given precedence over the needs of their individual child and that they were judged as bad parents.

Front-line education and social services workers also felt removed from the decision-making process. They would have liked to spend more time working with parents and acting as co-ordinators and advocates. The panels themselves usually had little opportunity to consider the needs of individual children; there were often disagreements between education and social services, inadequate information about children's needs and circumstances, and not enough time for a full discussion. Decisions could be delayed for many months.

4 Children's experiences of residential schools

We visited 32 disabled children and young people, using an information schedule developed in consultation with our Reference Group of young disabled people who were or had been at boarding school themselves. As explained in the Appendix, we were able to carry out semi-structured interviews with 14 children and young people. Interviews were not an appropriate method for gaining information about the experiences of the remaining 18. We therefore interviewed a support worker and/or teacher and also spent time with the child or young person at school and in the 'home' part of the school.

Involvement in decisions about placement

The majority of the children had gone away to school before the age of 11. We asked them whether they had a say in going to school. Some answered in terms of boarding school being the best way of meeting their educational needs. Peter had experienced great difficulties at his local mainstream school. He said, 'A school like this was the only option – otherwise I wasn't going to get an education.'

Anne said: 'At first I didn't want to go to boarding school. I visited a couple of schools to look at them. I didn't like the idea of boarding but I felt I had a say in whether I went.' Laura said that she had visited the school and thought she liked the idea of going there, although she hadn't realised how homesick she would be. She did feel, however, that she had a say in whether she went to boarding school. Krishnan said that he felt he had a choice about which school to go to.

Sometimes, a child was very clear that they were not happy with going away to school. Henry told us: 'I was ten years old. I have a picture of us on the [way to the school]. I was very homesick and crying a lot.' Carl was clear that he did not have a say in going to residential school:

> They just said to me that there was a school in [X] that I could be going to that most people, everyone there's got at least something a bit wrong with them and first of all I thought I might not get on with people there, then I thought, I'm going to miss my friends as well.

Some young people were keen to go to boarding school because of negative experiences in local mainstream schools. One of these was Jane, who spoke at the tribunal to decide her placement. They ruled that the authority should have taken account of Jane's preference. Neeta was very unhappy at her local school as she had no friends of her own age and wanted to be able to make friends with other Deaf young people. Her mother said that Neeta went for a weekend visit to see what she thought and came back and said: 'Mum, I've got 22 friends!'

Children and young people are of course influenced by parents or other important adults. Twelve-year-old Jacob took account of what his social worker and his mother said:

Jacob:	I visited and then I went back home again, and [the social worker] said it would be the right school for me.
Interviewer:	And did you think it would be the right school for you?
Jacob:	Yes.
Interviewer:	Why did you think that?
Jacob:	Because [the social worker] said it's nice, and the right school for you.

Some parents said that it was not possible to involve their children in the decision because of their level of impairment. Ben's parents had made some attempts to introduce him to the idea of boarding school:

> We kept saying, 'You are going to a new school, Ben', and he would sometimes look a bit sad and I took him up to the school and showed him the gates and we walked round and went in and out of the buildings and touched things.

However much children had a say in the decision to go away to school, and however much they saw the decision as being in their own best interests, most would still have rather been at home. As Peter said, he 'definitely' would have preferred to go to a local school – if it could have given him the education he now gets.

Feelings about being away from home

Almost all the children and young people who could communicate directly with us indicated that they had been homesick when they first went away. Suddenly finding yourself amongst strange adults and children can be very difficult. Peter highlighted this when asked whether he had been homesick. 'There's 60 boys and you don't know any of them, so it does take a few weeks to settle in.' Robert went to boarding school when he was ten, and remembered how difficult it was not knowing anybody. Neeta said she was 'very, very homesick' but that other students were really supportive and told her that everybody felt the same when they first came.

David talked about how he missed not just his parents but also his sisters, friends 'your possessions and everything … And everything that is at home is much more comfortable than anything else.' Comfort was a feature of home, contrasted with school, that a number of children mentioned. Carl described himself as a 'homeboy'. He had counted in years, terms and weeks how long he had left at school. He talked about home as a more relaxing and comfortable place: 'at home you can do almost what you like when you want. I get to relax. I get to just chill out and do my own thing at my own time.'

When a child's communication or cognitive impairment meant it was not possible to ask them questions, we tried to find out how they communicated their feelings in other ways. Sometimes the information came from staff. Adrian's keyworker described how he sometimes says 'I'm sad'. She said:

It's usually because he wants to go home. He'll say 'See Mummy' and I'll say 'Shall we phone Mummy?' and then afterwards I'll say 'Are you happier now?' and he'll say 'Happy'.

Gemma's keyworker said she had been very tearful when she first came and that it had taken a good six weeks for her to settle in, 'she would just burst into tears, quite hysterically at times'.

We were often told, by parents, support workers or by the children themselves, that what was most upsetting was seeing parents at school. Rosalie, for example, cried a lot when she saw her parents at her review meeting. Imtiaaz was very upset when his parents visited the school one day. The keyworker described: 'He just howled the whole time they were here, hid under the cushions.' The move from home to school could also be very hard for some of the children. Henry talked about having 'terrible nightmares' when he went back to school at the end of the holidays.

Some children and young people wanted to try to replicate bits of family life at school. Karen said that she liked that there weren't set or fixed activities in out-of-school time but that she could opt in or out of things: 'It's not like you have to choose one activity, you can stay in, you know, like in general families.'

Ryan said he felt more positive about being at school than being at home, although this was partly because his school sent students home for bad behaviour:

It became that school was so much better than being at home, I sort of started to resent being at home. One of the bad things that they did was that, if you did something wrong, they sent you home so they were basically using your home as a punishment. There were a lot of people resented their homes.

Being at school

Anne said she was pleased that she went to boarding school because:

> … my old school didn't give me what they give me at my new school … I get physio more often and this is good because I don't want to be bent all the time. That would mean I couldn't do what I want to do, I couldn't stand or stretch my legs. I need to be straight so I can do more stuff.

Ryan liked being at school because he said: 'Talking to my mates was like the best therapy I could have.' Sara, who communicates with body language, showed how much she liked people talking to her and being involved in the chat going on around her.

One boy said that his school put a lot of effort into how it presented itself to the outside world and he felt that this was sometimes more for show than for the benefit of the students:

> This school wins enough trophies for the best gardening or best this or that but I mean they do it when people are watching. When everyone goes the school is back to normal again.

The lounge that 12-year-old Jacob shares with other boys was a fairly bare room, the interviewer noted, with a table and chairs. However, his bedroom had lots of his own things in it – photographs of his family, and in his drawers he had the strip of his football team and other favourite items. The second time Jacob was visited, he had just moved into a new bedroom and it was newly decorated with colours he had chosen, with posters, photographs of friends, family, staff and himself on the wall. He had his own television and said he could watch what he liked. When asked 'Do you like it at this school?' he replied 'Yes I *do* like it at the school.'

Sometimes we were given conflicting messages about how young people were at school and how they experienced things. One interviewer noted Kate's obvious delight when her teacher used music to communicate with her. Later, the interviewer asked Kate's house-parent what she enjoyed doing:

House-parent: She doesn't like doing anything.

Interviewer: There's nothing that she positively enjoys?

House-parent: No. She has a very tentative relationship to life. She's a passenger. She won't look at a book, won't listen to music.

Laura communicated there was nothing she liked about being at boarding school. While her keyworker tried to insist that there *were* things that Laura liked doing, Laura herself was quite definite. She said she didn't like her room at school and neither did she really like the girl she shared with. She liked listening to music and watching television but could not always choose when and what to listen to or watch.

Education

The children participating in this research, like schoolchildren generally, had a range of both positive and negative experiences of education. Some children said they were very happy with the quality of the education they received. Sixteen-year-old Peter said: 'It's good, it's the best really. It's small classes and the teachers are all well qualified.' Some of his lessons only have four or five young people in them. Luke's classes had an even higher staff–pupil ratio, because the careworkers helped out in the classroom, together with teacher and learning support assistants. However, some children indicated that they didn't get the help they needed in the classroom. Laura said that she didn't get the help she needs in her favourite subjects, which are art and music. Her keyworker confirmed that Laura needed one-to-one help and that this was not always available in the classroom.

Neeta said she had a lot more work to do at her residential school than in her mainstream school back home. It was compulsory to do two to three hours' homework after school and she thought she was now getting a better education. Anne felt that the teaching was much better than at her old school:

> At my old school, I used to get told off for not listening, they never gave me a chance ... I get more help with learning at my new school. I'm reading and listening better. I'm more into the things they do – it's more exciting. I'm going to France on a school trip – I never went on a school trip with my old school. We've already been on lots of school trips, I went to sing in Westminster Abbey with the choir. My old school didn't have a bus I could get on.

In contrast, Ryan felt that his education in his previous, mainstream school had been better, although he was very unhappy there. He said that he enjoyed his time at residential school but felt that they gave him a lot of 'free rein'. Carl said his sister at school back home had more choice in the subjects that she could choose than him. One young person thought that the teachers shouted a lot apart from when Inspectors or visitors came to the school.

When we observed young people in their classroom, it was sometimes difficult to know what the teacher was trying to achieve and the young person or child often seemed unengaged with what was going on. We also observed situations where teachers moved from one activity to another without telling the children what was going on, and where classes were interrupted by visits from dentists and physiotherapists.

Often, young people with whom we could not communicate directly were on 52-week placements in order to benefit from a '24-hour curriculum'. We noticed, however, that classroom activities could sometimes have very little structure and could change very quickly without explanation.

Like all students, children and young people who we visited clearly had subjects and teachers they preferred over others. We noticed, however, that, for children without verbal communication, their responses and reactions in class were often 'explained' by teachers by referring to their mood that day, or to some health-related issue, or to bad behaviour rather than as an expression of choice and preference. Kate had been very happy in her first class of the day, but then moved to a basket weaving class. The interviewer noted:

> Almost immediately, Kate is less happy, she doesn't want to do basket weaving and the teacher doesn't seem able to engage with her as her last teacher had done. At one point Kate gets up and knocks over a chair. The teacher keeps saying, 'oh, isn't Kate in a bad mood today' … In the end Kate sits mostly alone not doing anything until lunchtime.

Evenings and weekends at school

Children had varying experiences of spending evenings and weekends at school. David said that weekends were good because he was allowed to go to bed later than during the week: 'But like, depending on our behaviour, staff can take so many hours off our bedtime.' However, weekends also sounded quite boring:

On weekends, there's not really a lot to do because, like, we do the same thing every single week. We get up late, have a lie-in, watch the TV, have our breakfast, get to synagogue, have a rest, have our lunch and for the rest of the day there are things that we are allowed to do like play ball games.

Jake said that he liked playing games on his computer but he didn't have these at school. He also did not have pictures of his favourite football team on his bedroom wall at school, although he did at home. Carl felt his free time at school was limiting and boring: 'There's hardly nothing fun to do. I can't enjoy myself.' He said there were 'strange rules' about what games they could and couldn't play. He was very into music but couldn't guarantee that he would get one of the tape recorders that the children had to share.

Sixteen-year-old Peter said that it was sometimes boring in the evenings as his school is in a small village and there is not much to do in the area. When he is at home, he goes to pubs and clubs but cannot do this when he is away at school. Rachel and the four other young people with whom she shares a bungalow all need a lot of help in order to go out and we were told that evenings are usually spent 'in' as there are not enough staff to go out. On the other hand, 16-year-old Henry – who does not need such a high level of support – seemed to have a lot of choice over what he did at weekends. He and the other young people he shares a house with go shopping, to the pub, to the cinema, to football matches, take part in sporting activities, and so on. Karen also felt able to choose what she did with her free time and would hang out, listen to music and watch TV: 'it's just like a normal house'. She worked on Saturdays for work experience. Both Karen and Ryan felt they had quite a lot of freedom and both of them enjoyed drinking. Anne had recently stayed at school for the first time at a weekend – 'I liked it', she said. 'I got more attention from the staff than they can give you during the week, so they could do things like go shopping with me. I'm going to stay again at a weekend because I liked it.'

However, in terms of what happens after school during the week, Anne would rather that there weren't so many organised 'activities'. She said she could choose what she does but 'I have to do something [and] I don't like having to do activities every day after school – I need a rest.' She wishes she could watch more television, which is what she does at home. Anne also really likes going out in the school grounds on her own in her electric wheelchair. This is the first time in her life that she has been able to spend time on her own outside in this way. She also likes just 'hanging around' with her friends. Neeta said there were lots of activities after school including opportunities to hang out with the boys. She had friends in a way that she hadn't had at home and at weekends they went shopping in town.

Going home

A small number of children on 52-week placements did not go home at all but got family visits at school. Almost all the children and young people who did go home were positive about going home. 'It's brilliant going home', said Henry, who also described being at home as 'a paradise'. Carl goes home every weekend and one of the things he liked best about it was the control that he had over his own time:

> I can play football any time, and I can listen to the radio. I can go to my room any time and just be quiet or put the radio on or the computer.

Rachel's mother described how Rachel was still very much part of her family, even though she had gone away to boarding school at the age of four. Although this was a 52-week placement, Rachel came home every weekend and for a fortnight every six weeks. When we visited Rachel at home, it was evident how she was central to her family. The house had been adapted to meet her physical needs and she spent a lot of time being held by her grandmother, parents or sister, sitting on the sofa. Rachel's main method of communication seems to be bodily tension and the high amount of physical contact she had with her family meant that they were better able to 'tune in' to her communication than the staff at school who were observed as having little physical contact with her other than to meet her personal care needs. For children like Rachel, we could not get a sense of what they felt about school and home without visiting them in both settings. Even though Rachel was visited at what her mother said was the 'sleepy time' of her day at home, the interviewer noted that she looked 'far brighter, more awake, relaxed and alert than she had done on either occasion' when she was visited at school.

Almost all of the children without verbal communication in this study clearly expressed their feelings about going home. Gemma's keyworker said: 'When her parents come to pick her up to take her home you can just see the light on her face.' Ben's mother told us:

> He does enjoy coming home. He bounces about like a kangaroo. His face lights up when he sees us so he really does appreciate coming back home.

The timing of visits home was mostly dictated by the school's routine and whether the placement was weekly, termly or 52 weeks. Robert was unusual in that, although each weekend was designated a 'home' weekend or a 'school' weekend, he could decide to go home on a 'school' weekend, and vice versa, if he wished. For other children and young people, choosing when to go home was not on the agenda.

When asked whether he had a say in when he went home, 18-year-old Krishnan said: 'It's like, if I'm good at home, I can go home.' Krishnan had a sense of how his behaviour was difficult for his parents to handle and Henry, too, said: 'I think I'm a bother being at home.' Some young people had turbulent relationships with their parents. Karen found home visits overwhelming at first because of difficulties with her mum and sometimes ran away. Now she finds them easier and worries that the time at home goes too quickly:

> I worried that my mum would shout at me and not want me home again if I had an overnight. But now … I'm mainly bothered about day visits going too quickly whilst an overnight visit you have time to get on and talk and all that.

David, aged 13, talked about wanting to spend more time with his father: 'I don't get to spend so much time with my dad.' This was partly because his father worked long hours but also because David himself was away at boarding school. He talked about what they did together: 'We go to the park, we build with Lego, play ball games, things just what most kids would do with their dads.'

There were things about school that some children missed when they were at home. David missed his careworker and his friends. Some young people who said that they loved going home also said it could be a bit boring at home. This was most often in the long summer holiday, especially if they had few or no friends in their home community.

Friends

For Anne, having friends was one of the main advantages of going to boarding school. She described how, at her mainstream primary school:

I just used to drive around in the playground in my wheelchair and [the other children] never used to come over to me. If I went over to them they would just go away. I've got loads of friends at my new school.

Some children described their experience of boarding school in terms of having closer friendships than they had had at a day school. David said:

Being with friends is like being with family, sometimes we get on really well, sometimes we quarrel a bit and other times, we make up, fall out again, make up, fall out, make up again.

Robert talked about how good it was being with other young people after school: 'We have a good laugh in the evenings.'

Ryan was one of the young people who said that they liked being at school with and friends with other disabled young people:

My friends at school we all used to talk about our problems and we realised we were having the same kinds of problems, we were all in it together. That was the best.

However, when someone leaves the school, the friendship can be lost forever. David talked about being very close to another boy who left the school: 'We used to be best, best, best friends.'

Robert recounted how he had a girlfriend at school but that the school didn't allow this: 'We had an assembly and they said we weren't allowed to have a girlfriend or a boyfriend. We had to keep it quiet.' Henry talked about not just wanting friends but also wanting a girlfriend. He had little social life during the holidays and obviously found this difficult. He described in great detail going to collect his sister from a church Christmas party during the holiday and seeing a girl he fancied: 'She has blue eyes like me, long hair and a red jumper … I spoke to her but forgot to tell her my name.' He also described how disappointed he was that an evening out bowling didn't result in making any new friends. His mother tries to find him friends during the holidays but he was quite lonely.

Anne's best friend at school lived about 300 miles away from her so they didn't see each other during the school holidays. She did, however, see her best friend from primary school when she was at home: 'We phone each other or she comes round.' Neeta kept in touch with her friends from school using texting and e-mail all through the holidays. Peter, aged 16, has no difficulty keeping in touch with his friends from school as they all live within the London area and can use public transport. He did, however, think that being at boarding school inhibited his opportunities to have a girlfriend:

It's quite difficult – if I'm at school for most of the year, a girl wouldn't really like it.

Some children and young people's closest relationships at school seemed to be with their keyworkers. Some keyworkers told us that young people preferred their own company. However, it was also evident that sometimes young people did not receive the assistance they needed in order to make and maintain friendships. For example, Laura, who uses a communication book, did not have the names of her best friends in the book.

Most of the children and young people had little contact with the wider community during term time. Sometimes this could be because of the reactions of other children; one keyworker described how, although the children were taken to the local park, they had no contact with other children playing there:

> We can clear the park with our children, there's only a minority of children who will stay and play when our children are there.

Staff

There were limits to how far we could get a clear view of how children felt about staff, in particular because many of them were interviewed with a support worker present. Some obviously felt inhibited by this. For example, when David was asked about whether children had any choice about who helps them, he said 'Ummmm … I don't really want to talk about that.' The support worker who was present offered to leave but he said she could stay if she wanted. On the other hand, David was positive about his keyworker and said that she had 'made an oath' that she would not leave the school until he did. Some children had had the same keyworker all the time they had been at the school; Adrian and Luke, for example, had had the same keyworkers for the last four years.

Rachel's keyworker had been with her for two years in primary school and continued with her when she moved up to secondary school. She had been to stay at Rachel's home and, according to staff, was Rachel's 'second mother'. Thirteen-year-old Anne asked a particular careworker to be 'my second mum. It was just something I thought of and she said "yes".'

We couldn't interview Luke (because of his level of learning disability) but we spent time with him and his keyworker and observed their close relationship. She talked about the 'boundaries' that the staff try to set on the children's behaviour but:

> ... he will do less for me than for other people because he knows he's my favourite ... People who aren't so loving towards him all the time get a better response from him ... he can manipulate me, I suppose. I'm a little bit too soft with him, probably like his mum is.

Some children said they had chosen their keyworker: 'The reason I chose [keyworker] – I thought she looked nice. She's head of house and talks a lot', said Henry. Neeta hadn't been able to chose her keyworker, but said that she got on really well with her and would be able to talk to her if she were sad or worried about anything. Karen, like several other young people, was assigned a keyworker but was able to choose another if she wanted. Carl had done this: 'Me, the reason I chose a man was 'cos all the time I've boarded here I had girls, or a lady, so I thought I'd make a change.'

There were situations we observed where there did not seem to be enough staff to meet the children's needs. Rachel, for example, needs one-to-one support, but the bungalow she lives in only has three staff for five young people, all of whom have similarly high levels of need. Luke's keyworker described the very difficult circumstances recently when the school took in more children and did not have enough staff to look after them properly:

It was just bedlam. This lounge is just the right size for four children but for eight it was awful … there should have been four staff in each lounge but it was a very good day if it did happen … you could get toys out or whatever but you didn't have enough time to focus on a child or anything … we had some pretty aggressive children here who needed one to one and two to one when they were blowing, then the attention is on them even from the staff who aren't working with that child, so Luke probably was sort of forgotten about when we were at our worst.

When a child or young person needs a high level of personal assistance, the way careworkers do things is very important. The majority of those who were able to tell us about their experiences told us that particular members of staff assisted them in ways that they did not like. There was only one instance, however, where a child was happy with the action which resulted from their complaint. This was Anne who talked about one careworker who she didn't like helping her –'She was horrible to me, she tried to hurry me up all the time' – and about how her mother wrote to the house-master and 'it got sorted out'. In other instances, children communicated that they did not have a veto over who helped them. Sometimes, staff seemed to put children's experiences down to 'a clash of personalities', as one keyworker put it. Rosalie communicated that she had told her keyworker that she didn't like a particular care worker helping her. The keyworker, who was present at the interview, said 'I think it sorted itself out' but Rosalie (who does not use speech) didn't look very happy about it. Laura had told her keyworker about a particular member of staff whom she didn't like helping her. The keyworker spoke to her line manager and the member of staff was due to have more training but was still working with Laura – who communicated that she was not happy about this.

When we couldn't ask children or young people about their keyworkers (because of their level of learning disability), we spent time observing the relationship. After spending the day with Gemma, the interviewer noted:

> Gemma's keyworker never spoke directly to her the whole day and made several negative comments about Gemma to me in front of her. The keyworker only had physical contact with Gemma when a task needed to be done. In contrast Gemma's previous keyworker, who had been her keyworker for the last two years and who still worked in Gemma's house, spent time sitting with Gemma on the sofa stroking her arm and chatting warmly to her. Gemma seemed to really enjoy this and seemed relaxed and happy.

Care workers sometimes treated children and young people with a lack of respect. An interviewer who had gone to visit Andrew observed one staff member saying to another, in Andrew's hearing, that Andrew was just like her 'dog, eager to wave, make contact with people, bounce up to them but unable to understand that was not the way to behave with strangers.' Sometimes we observed abusive behaviour. One young man was observed, in a standing frame, crying:

> All the students were having snacks and drinks. It was plain from the way that this young man's support worker spoke with him that she was fed up with him and didn't particularly like him. She approached him speaking brusquely and then forced some Kit Kat into his mouth, through his clenched teeth. Her movements were rough. She did this several times, all the time talking to him roughly and disrespectfully.

However, some staff put considerable effort and commitment into looking after the children they cared for. When Alan arrived at his current school, aged 12 and having been excluded from a previous school, he weighed three-and-a-half stone and his mother was frightened he would die. His support workers try to 'calm him down' before each meal and persist in trying to get him to eat. The interviewer was present during one meal time and noted:

> After one or two mouthfuls he would push the plate away, jump up and run out of the room. The support worker would follow him with another spoon (an 'indicator' for meal time). He would then come back, take a few more spoonfuls and be off again.

We observed Alan being carefully supported through a period when he tried to injure himself and how relieved his support worker was when he came through this:

> To show that he was very happy Alan started running up to the top of the stairs, standing there for a few moments and then ran down again. His support worker followed him, imitating his noises and the way in which he was jumping up and down with delight. She was visibly relieved to be doing this and clearly enjoying herself as she played this game with Alan.

Ben's keyworker was one of the few who saw Ben's 'difficult behaviour' as a positive way of him expressing himself. She said Ben had been very passive when he first came to the school:

> He was very calm and malleable – easy to dress, you know, will go with you easy. He was kind of very absent. Now he chooses his own clothes and puts them on. And with that sort of 'I'm much more here now' comes the provocative behaviour which I think is positive – it's definitely good.

Some children indicated that they got a lot of emotional support from their keyworker. Henry said: 'It's the best thing, talking to [keyworker] about wanting a girlfriend.' Some children wanted, and received, physical affection from their support workers. Imtiaaz's keyworker said, 'When you're walking along, he'll get you to bend down and give him a little cuddle.'

Adrian's keyworker takes him to visit her own family and he has become involved in her family's social life. She said: 'He'll visit my mum and he'll have his tea there. She gives him some pennies and he walks across the yard and he gets some chips.' 'Chips', said Adrian. 'Ketchup.' 'Yes, you like your ketchup. And she makes him some cake and sends it back for the other boys.' 'Cake', said Adrian. 'Sweets.' 'That's right', said the keyworker, 'the cake had sweets on top, didn't it?' She described taking Adrian to the funfair and they acted out for the interviewer what happened on the ghost train (Adrian had given her a fright).

Bullying

Few of the children talked about being bullied. Krishnan described being name called but had not complained about it.

Krishnan: B always laughs at my colour.

Interviewer: What sort of things does B say?

Krishnan: He says to me that I'm gay, he calls rude names to me sometimes. I don't really like it … some people laugh at me about my colour, I don't really like people laughing.

Interviewer: What sort of things are they laughing about?

Krishnan: My eyes, my everything, I don't really like it.

Rosalie communicated that an older boy had bullied her and that she hadn't told anybody about it. The keyworker present at the interview expressed surprise as she hadn't known.

Neeta said that there was a lot of 'bitchiness' at her school but not what she would call bullying. Carl was clear that bullying did go on at his school but that he had not been bullied: 'I wouldn't let anyone bully me.' Robert gave the impression that his school was good at dealing with bullying. He talked of some children who 'wreck our games' but said confidently: 'I told the teacher and the teacher told them off.' Robert also explained emphatically to the interviewer 'name calling *is* bullying', indicating this was something his school took seriously.

Cultural issues

Krishnan described how going back to India each year is important to him and that he has little contact with Indian culture at school although he listens to Asian radio. There is only one other student at his school who is of Indian origin. This aspect of Krishnan's experience was summed up by the following exchange:

Interviewer: So is it quite important to you and your parents that you keep in touch with India and your Indian culture?

Krishnan: I don't keep in touch here, I keep in touch at home.

Interviewer: So at home you have more of a sense of being Indian?

Krishnan: Yes.

Interviewer: And here you don't?

Krishnan: No.

One young man talked about feeling uncomfortable when he was taught to make a pizza with ham on it. 'That's pork isn't it?', he asked the interviewer. His family is Muslim and his parents were upset when he told them he had eaten ham. However, he had not felt able to tell the staff he shouldn't eat ham.

Other black children we talked to about what it was like to be at a school where most other students were white told us that it had not been a problem. Imtiaaz's keyworker described how she and the other workers cook the Indian food which Imtiaaz likes. His mother had told them what he likes and had also given them the recipes and advice about cooking the food.

A number of the children were at schools that were run by Christian organisations. They went to church every Sunday but weren't always very keen on this. Rosalie's keyworker talked enthusiastically about the children going to different churches in the area but Rosalie herself communicated that she didn't really like going to church. Henry had started confirmation classes but had decided 'I didn't want to carry on … That was up to me' and he didn't go to church any more.

Reviews

Review meetings can be intimidating and confusing, even to keyworkers. Luke's keyworker said: 'I find them terrifying. I don't like having to speak in front of more than one person and I've never got used to that even though I've been here eight years.' Henry said 'It's hard to explain to everyone in front of a group.' His mother said that he had been invited to come to the last two review meetings and he was 'very, very tense and anxious. And it was quite an ordeal for him.' He then refused to come to the next review meeting.

The majority of the young people who had been to their review meetings gave the impression that reviews were things to be endured and they weren't sure of their purpose:

Robert: You had to have them whether you liked them or not ... They were too long ... But I didn't say anything just listened.

Interviewer: Did you understand what people were saying?

Robert: A little bit.

Carl had been given his review papers in advance of the meeting and said he often disagreed with what was written about him:

> I went once, I said, 'I'm going this time to make things clear.' I don't know how, I mean they say I never help people. They say I don't like losing, that I have to expect it – but no one likes to lose. They say I'm selfish, I don't know how they can say I'm selfish. And they say I always like to put my opinions out which is true I have to admit.

Eighteen-year-old Krishnan was only called in at the end of his review meeting and recounted how: 'They said I was talking to strangers and that's got to stop, they said I could talk to old school friends but not strangers ... and meal times I've got to have at the right time.' It sounded quite an ordeal, being called into a meeting where everyone had been discussing him and then being told off.

Other children also described their review meetings in terms of people discussing whether they had done well or not. Anne said: 'I didn't like hearing about myself' when she attended her review meeting. She then chose not to attend the next meeting: 'I want to just find out from my keyworker.'

Thirteen-year-old Rosalie, who uses body language to communicate 'yes' and 'no', told us that she was invited into the end of her review meetings:

Interviewer: When you went to your review meeting, did people ask you what you thought?

Rosalie: Yes.

Interviewer: And did you say what you thought?

Rosalie: Yes *[very definite yes]*.

Interviewer: Did they listen?

Rosalie: No.

Conclusions

Most of the young people would not have chosen to go away to school, although some wanted to leave their old school because they were so unhappy there. Almost all said they were homesick when they went away and they missed a whole range of things about home – their family, but also their own space, their own things and their own routines. Going home is a highly enjoyable event for the majority of children, although a small minority of children did not go home at all.

Friendship was one of the most positive things young people told us about being at boarding school. Only a small number had active social lives and good friends at home as well. Some also felt they received a better education at boarding school.

Relationships with care workers were crucial to how a young person felt about being at school, especially for those with high support needs. Most, but not all, of the children were positive about their relationship with their keyworker. Most of them had also had difficulties with particular members of staff. We encountered a range of approaches from care workers towards young people. Some of it was excellent – warm, committed and engaged – but some was very dehumanising and showed very little respect.

5 Parents' experiences of residential schools

We asked parents about their experiences of their child being away at boarding school.

Parents' views on being separated from their children

The majority of parents spoke of going through a grieving process when their child first went away. Roy's mother felt 'begrudging as to the reasons why he had to go away', arguing that if they had had the right support it might not have been necessary. She thought she was doing the best for her child:

> I thought ... if I keep him at home I'm just thinking of myself, but if I send him to this school I'm giving him perhaps the only chance in life he's going to have. So I forced myself through that bereavement.

Sara's mother said: 'You have to be selfless enough to let go which is really hard to do. She was my baby.'

Parents talked of the initial trauma of separation. Jane's mother said: 'The first time she went she cried and I cried ... We had to pull over in the car because my husband and I were crying' and Nick's mother said: 'It was just terrible at first, he was clinging on to my legs and screaming.' Patrick's mother described feeling that 'I have made the biggest mistake of my life ... thinking "Just go and get in the car ... and bring him home. You are mad ... Why the hell is he there?"' Other parents talked of the guilt they felt. Ben's mother said: 'It is a very, very tough decision. The last thing you want to do is send your eight-year-old son away to a residential school. We still feel guilty.'

Some parents grieve every time their child goes back to school. Thirteen-year-old Rachel went away at the age of four-and-a-half. She comes home every weekend when her father makes the two-and-a-half hour drive to pick her up on Friday and take her back on Sunday night, and for two weeks every six weeks. Her mother said:

> I still cry after two weeks when I've had her home. I'm still standing at the doorstep crying my eyes out. And I don't think that'll ever change. I miss her very much … it's very wrenching but we have to do what we feel is best for Rachel as well as what's best for us.

She went on to describe what she thought were the benefits of Rachel being away at school:

> Rachel being at [school] makes it easier for us to function as a normal family, whatever normal families are. Because my husband can get on with his job during the week, I have time for my daughter for homework in the evenings, and then at weekends when Rachel's home we're a family and do things as a family, pictures, or go out … and I don't need respite because my respite is when she's at school and I can then cope during the two weeks when she's at home.

For some parents, the difficult and often acrimonious nature of the decision-making process meant that they had reached 'breaking point' by the time a placement was finally agreed. For a minority of our sample, their dominant emotions when their child went away were exhaustion and relief. One parent said: 'By the time she went we were a bit worn out with feeling too much anyway.'

A difficult time could be made harder if schools failed to arrange preparatory visits or did not get to know the child before they went. Ben's mother felt the school was unprepared for her son:

I said, 'You know we are handing our child over to you … and you don't even know him. You don't really know anything about Ben apart from what I have written down on the piece of paper.'

Some parents were very aware that their child could see their placement as rejection. When Henry reached 16, his mother thought his residential school's further education provision was better than the local college:

We eventually got him to agree to stay there. But he said to me at one point: 'You don't want me to come back. You don't want me.' It was awful really but obviously that is how he sees it.

Jack's mother had a similar experience:

> When he's in one of his bad moods … he will sort of throw in your face that he is only in residential school because you don't want him at home. Even though we try and explain to him the reasons behind it all … in fact Jack's weapon is that if I try to explain to him he will close his eyes so he can't see me signing so it is as good as saying 'Just go away. I don't want to talk to you.' Definitely it has affected our relationship without a doubt.

Most of the parents we interviewed had regular contact by phone with their child, once or twice a week. When the child could not talk on the telephone, the parent would usually ring and talk to them. Jacob's mother praised the way her son's school facilitated her contact and communication with him:

> I have access to Jacob all the time I want to. He phones me, we're in contact twice a week. He writes to me once a week and I write to him.

Communication with schools

Most parents were very happy with the relationship they had with their child's school. Contact with care staff tended to be at least once a week, either through telephone calls or, if a child went home at weekends, a book was sent with them with written communication between school and home, and vice versa.

Rosalie's mother described the school's response to when Rosalie had fallen out of bed one night, grazing her skin quite badly:

They were marvellous. The people who were working that night rang me, they told me what had happened, they were in tears. It was genuine … it was awful it happened and they said: 'Do you want us to take this further?' and I said: 'No, as long as her bed was safe' … and when [her escort] took her back on the Sunday they took her up to her bedroom and showed her what they had done that weekend; [there was a] beautiful quilt Winnie-the-Pooh which is her favourite, all padded around … and they rang me a couple of times a week after that to see if I was OK, reassuring me that Rosalie was fine.

Some parents had developed close relationships with their child's keyworker. Adrian had had the same keyworker for four years (ever since he started at the school) as had Luke, whose mother said: 'I'm really good friends with his keyworker … she phones me at least once a week.' Rachel's keyworker had stayed at the family home.

Henry's mother found that communication between herself and the care staff was good but that she had little contact with the teachers. She found it difficult that the school did not have 'open evenings' and that the only opportunity to find out how Henry was doing was at the Annual Review meeting. More recently, she has had better communication with the school because one particular teacher is now liaising with her and telephones her:

She would ring me up at about 8 o'clock when she knew we would be home and she would talk to you. She would say: 'He is doing this and he is doing that' and just talk to you in general and it was very reassuring.

Some parents had negative experiences of previous boarding schools, which often led to the collapse of the placement. Owen's mother described her protracted dispute with her son's previous school: 'We had lots of meetings. The lady who was in charge of care had everything in her book, if it wasn't in her book it didn't exist.' Things did not improve and soon afterwards Owen injured himself. Owen's mother contacted her local authority to complain and, as a result, an Inspection team went into the school. The school said: 'he's just got to leave and they said if I don't come and pick him up then they're going to call the police in to take him away and have him sectioned. It was just terrible.'

Communication between school and parents was often most fraught when there were difficulties with a child's behaviour. Ryan's school sent him home as a punishment which his mother found confusing: 'They sent him home for a week, we said, "well, he was sent to a special school because we thought you would be able to cope with him. If he was easy to cope with we wouldn't have sent him away."' On another occasion, the school told her that he was being sent home as a punishment and then changed their mind without letting her know: 'I was angry. I spoke to the headmaster and told him … they had let Ryan down and he said: "perhaps we ought to think about another placement".'

Some parents and their local authorities felt, as one education officer put it, 'held to ransom' by schools who say, 'Well if you don't like it, try finding somewhere else'. A social work team leader spoke of the parents of a 14 year old who felt 'powerless to do anything … because there's nowhere else for him to go. They wouldn't want to rock the boat at school … They know they can't manage him at home. It's the final option, if that falls through, what do you do next?'

Sometimes, parents said, it could be hard to work out when the school would make a decision about things and when the parent would, and what to do if there was disagreement. When Owen's mother was in dispute with her son's previous school, the school told her she was 'interfering and difficult to work with':

> I told them straight, I had full parental responsibility and what parent would want to see her child in that state. Even though he's a 52-week placement, he's still our son and we still want to keep in touch with him, even though we can no longer look after him. I mean you don't just put him away and forget about him.

Nick's mother felt 'strange' about the fact that, when she went out with her son on days out from school, his careworker had control over Nick's money:

> She goes and pays for everything out of Nick's money, which is very nice, don't get me wrong, but where's all the money coming from, I don't know and to me that's strange – I'm his parent and he's not in care or anything.

A social work team leader reflected on the challenges that parents face, especially when their child goes to a 52-week placement. She spoke about a father who had 'struggled for many years as a single carer' and is now:

> … trying so hard to keep involved with this young boy and education only provide up to six journeys a year … And this dad obviously wants to see him much more and we're helping him with petrol money. I think he's struggled with it quite a lot and he's wanting to have his son home for a little holiday but he's been told: 'well, it's a little early, let him settle, don't have him too much to begin with', so he feels that he's being, not exactly told what to do, but he's trying to please the school, and be seen to work with them. In the end, he'll probably go along with what the school says. This is a ten-year-old boy who has lived at home with his dad all his life up until now.

Some of these issues are connected with some parents working through what it means for their child to be a 'looked after child' and we will look at this in more detail in the next chapter.

Review meetings

Henry's mother found annual review meetings unhelpful. She felt 'talked down to and patronised'. The meetings were not informative but seemed to be:

> ... more kind of 'We do this here. This is the way we do things here.' And they expect you to say 'Oh yes, that's lovely. That's wonderful.'

Some parents were more committed to going to reviews than others. Kieran's mother said: 'Mostly one of us goes but you know most of it already so it's like going through the motions.'

A number of parents thought that schools were very good at involving children in their reviews. Jacob's mother said:

> I've been to two reviews at [the school] now and the first thing to say is that Jacob is included in his review and I found that gobsmacking the first time – he's being treated as a person. And he sat beautifully on both occasions and they asked for his thoughts.

In contrast, Karen's mother was very unhappy that her daughter came to her reviews:

I don't agree that I should have to discuss my feelings and thoughts about my daughter while my daughter is sat there. I think I should have the opportunity to speak to all the professionals on their own … then we bring Karen in and we tell her what we've talked about, what decisions we've made and we give Karen a chance then to put her point across.

The experience of review meetings could be heavily influenced by the involvement of LEA and social services representatives, and this is discussed in the next chapter.

Parents' views on whether schools met their children's needs

Parents generally had more to say about their children's social, emotional and care needs than the quality of their education, although some felt the two were inextricably linked and a few praised the standard of education. Jack's parents, for example, felt that he really benefited academically from being in a small class of five children with one subject teacher who uses BSL and a classroom assistant.

Many parents talked of the importance of a school's ethos or atmosphere. Nick's mother appreciated the open and rural environment and the staff's approach:

Nick's keyworker was great – like an old hippy and Nick gets on great with people who are laid back. The school was beautiful, in the mountains … and they were really good with him. And he seemed at home.

Keyworkers were crucial. Sara's mother thought that her daughter's keyworker didn't have the right approach:

> [She's] a bit soft with her. Sara thrives on, 'right come on then'. No amount of namby pamby gets you anywhere with Sara.

Patrick's mother had wanted a gentle spirited person for his keyworker, but was very disappointed with the one who was allocated:

> Lots of them are nice mumsy types, like from the Ambrosia rice advert, and the others are young girls who are really sweet and ... enthusiastic ... But she is ... [a] disciplinarian, authoritarian, bombastic, horrible, bossy bitch.

A few parents talked about the advantages of the school having specialist knowledge. Rosalie's mother appreciated the enthusiasm of an information technology teacher. Using a communication aid, Rosalie could, for the first time, communicate in sentences rather than just indicating 'Yes' or 'No'. However, the school cannot provide Rosalie with her own piece of equipment, so 'she has her turn which is maybe an hour every so often'. Her parents have been told that they would need to raise £10,000 to buy one, so they have started fundraising.

Anne's mother talked of how the school 'will take on your battles'. She felt Anne's local school had looked to her for advice and support about Anne's needs – 'and I wasn't qualified to give it. Whereas now I've got the school to advise me and they offered to sort things out for me.' She also felt that Anne had benefited greatly from the way physiotherapy was integrated into the school day: her balance had improved, she had increased her ability to do things with her hands and contractures in her knees had been prevented.

Like a number of other parents, Robert's mother felt that her son's relationships with his peers were an important part of his boarding school experience. Anne's mother said:

> It's been amazing to me how important that is … People aren't friends with her because they're being kind … she's got the mobility because the whole site is accessible … she's not dumped in a corner and people have got to come to her … They've all got problems and they all respect each other's problems and they know about them and they understand them and they're very supportive of each other's problems.

Some parents, whose child's behaviour was a major issue, felt that a school's approach was more positive than that of their local school. Jacob's mother said: '[At his local special school], he wasn't getting educated because they were spending all their time dealing with his behaviour.' In contrast: '[His current school] are yet to be negative about him … Obviously they want to help him and they want to modify his behaviour but they accept Jacob and they accept this is part of Jacob.'

Ben's parents wanted the school to address Ben's 'obsessions' and for him to acquire skills around dressing and eating. They felt the school had been successful on both fronts: 'The difference in a short period has been amazing really.' Kate's parents wanted her to be able to do more for herself and for her to have fewer temper tantrums. They thought the 'quiet, peaceful, but not stark' atmosphere at the school was just right. '[Kate is] a different person since she has been at residential school … more often than not she is a pleasure to have around.' Neeta's mother spoke of how having friends had made all the difference to her daughter's behaviour:

> Before, she wouldn't do as she was told, she was always looking for attention, but it was all the result of being in the wrong place. She's not like that now. She's the total opposite.

However, some parents were not happy with a school's approach. Patrick's mother thought the school didn't display sufficient insight or expertise about his impairment. She had thought her son would benefit from what she understood to be a '24-hour curriculum'. Yet, when she spent the first week at the school with him:

> … the reality was much more chaotic than I imagined. There were loads more people. I said to one of the care staff, 'is someone supposed to be with me and Patrick and, if so, how long will that person be with us for?' And she said, 'Oh we usually spend half an hour with the child and then we swap around and go on to another one.' And I thought, 'God, he's only just got here and you want him to deal with a change of face every half hour.' When I asked the Head of Care if perhaps we could have a small group of people who were going to be working with me and Patrick, co-ordinating Patrick's integration, she said, 'Oh yes, that's a good idea' … I thought … no, please, don't let it be me halfway through the week to suggest this and you then go, 'that's a really good idea'. Please let someone else be in control. Please let someone else know what they're doing. I don't want to be the one with the good ideas.

The children of two of the parents interviewed were at a school which received a very critical report from the local Inspection Unit and subsequently closed. In both cases, the parents said the report came as a 'shock' and as a 'surprise'. 'I felt he had been getting the care although I knew that other children had been attacking him', said Adrian's mother. However, she had had some concerns and had asked a social worker to visit him at school and had herself been 'doing spot visits'. On two or three occasions, she said, she had wanted to take him out of the school: 'What stopped me was there's been no support when I've had him at home.' She went on to talk about Adrian's experience of verbal and physical abuse. Adrian imitates other people's behaviour and when he comes home, she said, he role-plays someone saying 'little shit', 'little git', 'bastard' and kicking someone on the ground. His mother said:

> We try to toughen Adrian up, tell him to run. He's going to get it throughout his life … A lot of the time he's just in the wrong place at the wrong time.

Luke's mother said that, in spite of the Inspection report, 'I wanted him to remain there, desperately', although she also said she had very mixed feelings about it:

> Part of me thinks I should be taking him out straightaway … but I know that [his keyworker] genuinely adores Luke and is looking out for him … the bit of the school where Luke is there's super staff that have been there for years – care staff and teachers. And Luke has done so well there, he's a lot calmer … I want to keep him there because I don't want him to have another change in his life, he's done so well I don't want to set him back at all. But then part of me is thinking am I being a bad parent by letting him stay there when this awful report came out?

Cultural issues

Issues relating to race and culture only came up in interviews with parents in terms of religion. Jacob at first attended a Jewish boarding school but his mother and his social worker were not happy with the way he was treated there. His mother reluctantly agreed to a move to a non-Jewish school but has been pleasantly surprised by the way they have met his religious needs, even though he is the only Jewish child there:

> I very much wanted Jacob to remain in a Jewish environment. He's going to be bar mitzvahed next year … [the school] has accommodated this unbelievably and so he's not going to miss out on this. He's being bar mitzvahed here but he's going to be supported up there … I bring him home for the most important Jewish holidays and he's now attached to a local Jewish community in [the nearest town] and someone takes him every other week to Hebrew school, sometimes one of the Hebrew teachers comes to the school and my [Jewish] director of education has done a tape and various people have been given a copy and so people are helping him go through whatever he has to do. He's not going to be doing very much but he's going to be singing some blessings and saying a prayer and they are very thoughtful about that.

A number of the schools were run by Christian organisations and this was an important part of their ethos. Most parents were happy for their child to attend Christian assemblies and go to church, although religion was rarely an important part of the parents' lives. One exception was Ben's parents: 'It seemed very good and we explained that we are a Christian family and very much felt that God led us there and there was a very definite "God-held" view there.' Another exception was Krishnan's parents who are Hindu and were 'a little bit concerned because [the school] is a Catholic school'. They had raised the issue with the headteacher and he had said, according to Krishnan's father that, 'he is keeping this in mind'. Krishnan's father went on to say: 'I don't mind if they teach about religion, but if they was just teaching Catholicism and not other religions I would object.' Krishnan's mother said: 'When he comes home, we go to temples and we have our religious festivals in August so he can still participate in that … and he came home in term-time for a religious festival in October.'

Jack's family are Catholic but Jack has not been able to make his first Holy Communion because he is at a non-Catholic school. While he could have gone to a catechism class on Saturdays (he boards weekly), his mother would have had to go with him in order to act as his Sign Language Interpreter and she could not do this because of 'the pressure of the family'. It was important to Jack's mother that her children attended Catholic schools but she felt that she had to put Jack's need for a signing environment first.

Holidays

Not all children and young people went home either at weekends or for holidays, though most did. Whilst there were issues and concerns relating to levels of support for families when their child came home, there was also delight at having their son or daughter home. Neeta's mother told us that it was 'lovely' when Neeta came home for holidays: 'I can't wait for her to come home and she has this big beaming smile when she sees me.' For others, the pleasure was mixed with feelings that it could be difficult having their children at home again. Ben's mother said:

> It's a real shock to the system … because you have sleepless nights again and you are running round all over the place all the time trying to keep an eye on what he is up to and you can't really do a lot with him at home but we are always very sad when he goes back.

Lack of support once a child had gone to residential school was a big issue for some parents. Roy's mother felt that the social services department 'forget you exist because you fell off the edge of the planet because you're now out of borough and they all sigh with relief that you don't exist any more. It took me years to unpeel that one, to get help in the holidays.' Patrick's mother found her local sources of support connected with her son's local special school and respite unit ceased once Patrick went to boarding school: 'I feel like the carpet has been pulled from underneath my feet.'

Some parents were reluctant to ask for help in the holidays or at weekends, and some said that social services had a 'punitive' attitude towards them. Parents had got what they wanted – residential school – so they couldn't also expect help when they wanted their child at home. A social worker illustrated this when asked whether any support was being offered to Kate's family when Kate came home:

> No. I mean the deal was that if Kate was going to a residential school then, as far as I was concerned, she wasn't having any respite as well, because that was not the option.

Some parents acknowledged that their children got bored in the long holidays and were ready to go back to school. Henry's mother said:

> He is totally isolated in the holiday and normally that hadn't worried me … but now he said 'I want a friend' and he got to the point of leaning out of the window and trying to attract the attention of passers by.

His mother rang local organisations but has not managed to find anything that Henry could go to during the school holidays. Jack had been given information about a coaching week for disabled children being run by a premier league football club, but when he went he was the only Deaf boy there and he refused to go again. His mother said he felt inhibited about going anywhere where young people of his age are, because he worries that he will be the only Deaf young person and everybody will stare at him.

Many parents experienced difficulties sorting out travel arrangements for their child to come home for holidays or at weekends. There were also problems relating to getting financial help to visit their children at school. We will look at this in the next chapter.

The future

A residential school placement did not mean that everything was settled. Indeed, the majority of parents were living with a lot of uncertainty.

Ryan was excluded from school and it was unclear what was going to happen next. One mother said she thought it was only a matter of time before her child was either killed by someone, or killed themselves. Patrick's mother was unsure boarding school was right for her son and was thinking about bringing him home. Gareth's school was threatened with closure but his mother did not want him to move. Two of the children's school closed down and they had to move to another one.

School-leaving age brought new worries. Nick was nearly 17 and his mother was searching for a college closer to home. Jane's parents had found a college they wanted Jane, now 18, to go to but it was no closer to home than her school.

Local education authorities could also create uncertainty. Kate's placement was reviewed every academic year by her local authority, which would only commit to it financially one year at a time. Her parents found this stressful.

A few parents never become reconciled to their child being away from home. Rosalie's family was planning to move so that Rosalie could become a day pupil. 'I didn't want a residential school. I wanted her to go to a day school.' On the other hand, some parents felt that their son or daughter would never come back to live full-time at home. This was particularly so if their child's behaviour was difficult to live with, and they believed that, if their child came home, the support the family needed would not be provided. Some parents also felt that being away at school had given their child an independence that was positive and should be maintained.

6 The involvement of education and social services authorities after placements are made

Education authorities

The responsibilities of education authorities

While there has been a general increase in joint or tripartite funding of recently made placements, in three of our four case study areas the majority of *existing* placements were still funded solely by education. In two areas, the majority of placements made during the year in which our research was carried out (2000) were education-funded placements, while, in one area, there were no joint-funded placements during that year. This reflects the general picture from the first stage of our research where joint-funded placements make up more than half of all placements in only 20 per cent of authorities (Abbott *et al.*, 2000).

The statutory responsibilities of local education authorities, following a placement in an out-of-authority school, are confined to an annual review of the child's Statement of special educational need; a referral to social services of all placements that involve the child staying at school for a consecutive period of more than three months (Section 85 of the Children Act 1989); and a referral to social services of all children for whom a residential placement is being considered:

> ... to ensure that a parental request for residential education is not made on the basis of lack of support and practical help in their local community and that proper arrangements are made to ensure family contact if the child is placed outside the authority in question.
> (Education Act 1993, Code of Practice on the Identification and Assessment of Special Educational Needs, para. 119)

The first stage of our research found little awareness amongst 21 local education authorities of their responsibilities under Section 85 of the Children Act and a general assumption that social services departments would know about the children anyway (though this was not by any means always so). This was also the situation in our four case study areas.

We asked the four education departments how they monitored care standards where there was no social services involvement in arranging or supporting the placement. One senior education officer said that she relied on the annual review. 'Part of [the educational psychologist's] assessment is about how are things going generally, and an interview with the child to see how things are going.' She said that 'the psychologist is looking at the needs of the child as a whole and will be asking the child "How are you getting on generally?", not just "How are you getting on with reading?"'. However, she confirmed that the largest group of children placed in residential placements have 'severe learning disabilities' and would not be able to participate in such a discussion. Moreover, the pro forma used for the annual review by this authority does not include questions about care. In another authority, the senior educational psychologist said that there was a checklist for his colleagues to use when they did visits to schools but 'Often you get a bit of scrappy paper coming back and you're never sure if they've done the checklist.'

Some education professionals expressed concern at the limitations of their role:

> We don't have a social services framework for scrutiny when it comes to welfare ... I've certainly been to visit schools in the past and was not happy and spoke to various people but it didn't go anywhere.

An educational psychologist pointed out that they were not 'caseholders':

> We place a youngster at residential school. That doesn't mean we necessarily carry on with that youngster.

Education officers were often quite clear that their role was fairly minimal once a child was placed out of the area. As one said:

> Everything is organised by the school and we just go along once a year, so we aren't involved with the child for the rest of the year … we appear … and report back to our authority what's happened at the review. But really, once they're in a residential school, the school does everything.

A senior educational psychologist acknowledged that it was possible that no one from a placing authority would go to the school for a couple of years:

> It's very worrying but … there are other pressures about what we're doing with *our own youngsters* [our italics]. What about the schools we've got failing, the number of statemented children we have got to service and so on? And, at some point, the line needs to be drawn and that's how we've drawn it.

Annual reviews

Only in a small minority of cases was an education representative present at each annual review and, for a few children in our study, there was never anyone from the education authority at the annual review of their Statement. A social worker in one case study area talked of three children on his caseload at boarding schools, where no one from the education department turned up for the annual reviews. In one authority, the education department had a policy that it would only attend out-of-area reviews at key stage transfers. This was in part so that the authority could think again about whether the child still needed to be in an out-of-area placement and also a recognition that they did not have the resources to go every year.

Some educational psychologists felt that attending annual reviews was not that useful anyway:

> You turn up and the school has scheduled ten reviews that day so you get half an hour for a review and you just rush through it, no time to talk to anybody and you rush off because your train is at 3.30. And do we keep doing that just to make sure, actually, they're still alive because I've seen them and that's basically all you do.

When educational psychologists do attend reviews their involvement is sometimes very much appreciated by parents. Roy's mother described how, at his last annual review – which followed a very difficult time – 'the EP came up with some really positive suggestions and they're working.' She had been worried that Roy's behaviour might lead to his exclusion. Having the educational psychologist at the review meeting and having her understanding of the issues for Roy was crucial: 'The EP is the one that the school listen to the most.'

On the other hand, some parents had found attendance at the annual review by a representative of the local education authority to be at best unhelpful and at worst very worrying. Peter's mother complained that the senior educational psychologist who attended her son's annual review 'behaved as if it was his own money that was being spent on the placement and he carries on giving the message that it's all costing too much money ... he makes me quite anxious.'

Parents also felt anxious about people coming from the authority who they had never met and who had never met their child. This concern was shared by some education professionals. An educational psychologist told us: 'I've never known a child whose review I've been to.' In another authority, a senior educational psychologist said:

> We seem to pass around annual reviews like a party game at the moment. It's not our current practice that an EP who starts off with a family will stay with them and see it through.

Supporting parents

Our initial study of 21 local education authorities found that they did not seem to view encouraging contact between parent and child as part of their role, and this was confirmed by our four case study areas and by parents. When Rosalie started school, her parents assumed that she would be coming home every weekend and arranged this with the authority's transport service. However, after the first term, Rosalie's mother received a phone call saying that Rosalie would have to start staying at school at the weekend and only come home at half-terms and for school holidays. When Rosalie's mother challenged this she was told that the authority was paying for a termly rather than a weekly placement and that 'We will be withdrawing transport.' The parents managed to negotiate that Rosalie comes home every alternate weekend.

Practices concerning assistance with transport varied quite widely and seemed to depend on what individual parents asked for. One parent claimed petrol money for her trips to her daughter's school over 100 miles away, yet others in the same authority received no financial assistance. Some parents were reluctant to ask for additional help for fear of 'rocking the boat' and others felt that the local authority's attitude was rather punitive. Patrick's mother had a long struggle to get agreement to a 52-week placement and, when she queried whether the local education authority would fund more than one trip home a month, she was challenged as to whether a 52-week placement was appropriate. Kate's parents were told that it was their responsibility to take her to and from the school where she was a weekly boarder 'because it was our choice that she went to that school'.

None of the four local education authorities participating in this stage of the research had an explicit policy of supporting parents to go to annual reviews. Individual officers told us that they sometimes offered a lift to parents but the general attitude seemed to be the one that was expressed by the chair of one authority's Learning Support Panel, who said:

Our view is that our budget is to support statemented pupils, it's not to help parents get to meetings. We expect parents to attend annual reviews under their own steam because they agreed for the child to go to the residential school.

Some parents may need other help – such as interpreters – in order to be involved in an annual review, but it seemed that local education authorities do not see this as their role either. A social worker for Deaf children told us of arguments between education and social services as to who has responsibility for sign language support to Deaf parents – with neither department accepting responsibility: '[the parent] will ask us for funding and we will say, "No it's an education issue it's not a social work issue".'

Relationships with the children and young people

Education professionals in the four case study areas did not generally have ongoing relationships with disabled children and young people at boarding schools, which again reflects a finding of our earlier study of 21 authorities. There seemed little expectation that they would seek out the views of children on their placement, and this was especially true if the young person in question had a communication impairment. Parents and staff were relied upon for information and it was often felt that education professionals did not have enough time to know how a child was really doing. As a senior educational psychologist said:

Ideally … they would want to meet the child [but] the approach is different if the child doesn't communicate verbally … [they] tend to rely on staff … and on parents … To know what was really going on you'd have to stay for a couple of days.

Procedures for keeping track of the service being purchased seemed under-developed. As one senior education officer said: 'We had started to develop a contract for schools but the person doing that work has left and it hasn't been taken up by anyone else yet.' Sometimes, difficulties in a placement were reported to learning support panels, or to joint or tripartite panels, but these did not seem effective mechanisms for addressing problems. One example concerned a child with a diagnosis of autistic spectrum disorder whose placement was discussed over a period of three months at panel meetings at which we observed. Concerns were expressed by an educational psychologist about the difficulty he had getting access to the school, uncertainty about whether annual review recommendations were being carried out and worries about the child's medication and standard of care received. Three months later, the panel received a child psychiatrist's report saying that the child should be moved as a matter of urgency. However, the social worker and mother were reported to be happy with the placement, the panel had not been able to find an alternative, and it was decided to see what happened at a joint visit to be arranged between education and social services.

Social services authorities

The responsibilities of social services authorities

If a social services department is involved in arranging a placement, the child has 'looked after' status and there is a duty under the Children Act 1989 to draw up a care plan, to review it at regular intervals and to visit the child regularly. Social services authorities also have responsibilities towards 'children in need' (and disabled children come under this definition) to 'promote the upbringing of children by their families'. There is also a responsibility to enable disabled children to lead 'as normal a life as possible' (Children Act 1989, Schedule 2, para. 6).

Our earlier study of 21 social services authorities indicated that few were consistently and constructively using Children Act regulations to protect the interests of children at residential schools. Neither were they always helping parents to maintain their relationship with their child. This finding was confirmed by our more detailed look at four case study areas.

One of the main reasons for the lack of consistency was confusion about whether Children Act regulations applied to children at boarding schools, although, even when a child *was* formally recognised as 'looked after', they were rarely accorded the full protection of the Children Act. Only one of our four case study authorities was clear that, when social services was involved in arranging a placement, this created obligations under the Children Act. A senior manager from this authority said: 'If a child receives overnight respite [*sic*] at a Resource Centre, then they're looked after, so of course out-of-county placements are looked after.' He pointed out that: 'It's highly unlikely that someone would move into an external placement if they weren't already in receipt of substantial amounts of service from us, including overnight stays, so they would already be looked after.' He also went on to say the authority had been applying this policy for the last seven or eight years: 'We wanted to make sure they were part of the Children Act reviewing system. It isn't just the fact that they're a major expense, it's also to make it clear these are cases for whom we have significant responsibility.'

However, as discussed in Chapter 3, this authority also sees this policy as a 'deterrent' (in the words of the senior manager) to parents who ask for a social services contribution to a residential placement. As the same manager pointed out, the children who are placed in boarding schools are very likely to have already been in receipt of short-term placement (respite) services outside their home and will therefore already be treated as 'looked after'. It is only because parents do not realise this that the status can be used as a 'deterrent' to put them off pursuing a boarding school placement for their child.

Within the three other authorities, there were many different views on legal responsibilities towards children at residential schools. One team leader said that any jointly funded placement carried 'looked after' status, while another team leader in the same authority said this would apply only if it was a 52-week placement. In another authority, a team leader said that a jointly funded placement only acquired 'looked after' status 'if they are away from home for 120 nights a year', a statement which is based on a misunderstanding of the regulations applied to short-term placements.

One social worker with five children at boarding schools on his caseload said that only the one who had been subject to a care order was really 'looked after' but that he still treated the other four as 'accommodated' (i.e. 'accommodated' by the social services authority and therefore having 'looked after' status): 'There were no issues around child abuse … but I treat them all in exactly the same way. In terms of visits, I like to see them four times a year, for example.' In contrast, his team manager was of the view that even children on 52-week placements were not 'accommodated', although, as she pointed out: 'This is a bit illogical as, if they have respite during the holidays at [residential respite unit], we treat them as "looked after".' She went on to say:

> When we started placing children in boarding schools we were concerned that no one was looking after these children, why weren't we treating them the same as other placements? So, we sought legal advice and were told that you don't have to regard them as 'accommodated' children but you must visit them as if they are 'accommodated'.

Within the same authority, but in another social work team, the response was slightly different. 'No, we don't treat any of ours as "looked after"', said the senior manager, who also went on to explain:

> We thought we were treading on thin ice so we actually got counsel's opinion and I know that the view is that we do not have to 'accommodate' the children we've funded as 'looked after'.

On the other hand, another authority had received counsel's opinion that a child, funded by social services, *was* 'looked after' and 'accommodated' by the authority and that therefore Children Act regulations applied. Social workers and managers told us that, even if a child is 'technically' classed as 'looked after', social services' involvement varied according to their assessments of parental involvement and capacity:

> When the parents are fully involved we are much less involved, which I think is right; it's not our role to take things over because it's a real shock for parents to realise that their child is being taken into care.

For most of the parents interviewed, the terms 'looked after' and 'accommodated' meant nothing and they could not remember anyone having explained that the social services authority might have responsibilities concerning their child's welfare. Others remained confused about what the situation was. Ben's parents were asked whether social services had talked about Ben being 'looked after':

Ben's mum: In the care of social services do
                                    you mean? I had to sign his care
                                    over to social services because he
                                    is sleeping away from home for
                                    such a large portion of the year ...

She just sort of went through the form with me and I signed it to say about part responsibility for decisions by social services. Obviously, that was quite big as well because you are sort of handing over half the responsibility to outside people. They can make decisions as well but obviously we have the main say.

Ben's dad: I think we still get to make the decisions.

Ben's mum: We don't – it's half and half basically.

Ben's dad, to interviewer: What is your understanding of that? Have we understood that correctly?

Some social workers, in explaining what 'looked after' status meant, were sensitive to parents' feelings: 'I'm pretty straight with them and say they're the parents and they'll always be the parents and they have parental responsibility.' Other social workers had limited sympathy:

I've had to explain it very carefully to some parents and they're shocked by it. Some parents are just fine and wouldn't think about it and others, I don't want to be judgemental, but high-income, middle-class parents, they want a lot of questions answering.

Karen's mother objected to her daughter being a 'looked after' child. She felt it relegated her role as a parent and gave her daughter the message that she was in care:

The 'looked after' is just another way of saying 'in care' and I object to that. I really, really object to it and it comes up at every meeting. I object that whatever happens to my daughter there is a list they follow, a pecking order and why am I not at the top of that pecking order? If there are decisions to be made, why am I not number one? It's very, very important that Karen knows that she's not in care. And she does think she's in care because of the language they use.

Relationships with children and young people at residential schools

Social workers often told us that lack of time prevented them building up a relationship with a child at boarding school: 'I feel that we get more and more distanced from children … you used to have more chance to see them and work up a relationship – you don't get the chance for anything like that now.' This was especially the case if the child had a communication impairment. In these instances, social workers sometimes said that they felt it was preferable for them to talk to somebody else about the child in question: 'Within the boundaries on my time, there are some children I can't communicate with and it's more honest to say that.'

However a few social workers put a lot of time and energy into their relationships with children. One social worker, who was unusual in that she visited children regularly, said:

> At the end of the day, I have sleepless nights over some of our placements ... you worry about them because you can't be there 24 hours a day ... And you go in and it's your gut instinct at the time about whether they're happy and have got relationships with the staff. You're the worker and when things go wrong, at the end of the day, you're the one that sees the child ... and it's quite a lot to bear on one worker.

Supporting parents

It seemed that supporting parents to maintain contact with their child did not figure very highly on the agenda of the social workers in our study, if at all. Social workers tended to give the impression that any support would either be on an ad hoc and informal basis – such as offering a parent a lift when going to a review – or would only be provided if there was pressure from a parent: 'It's not automatic but, if there's any difficulty, it would be looked at', said one social worker.

We found that parents were often reluctant to ask for financial help with the cost of travel to the school, yet social workers said that they thought that parents didn't want help because they hadn't asked: 'Often you'll find the parents won't even ask us anyway; they think it's their child so they'll go anyway as any of us would.'

Social workers within the same authority took varying views on, for example, whether or not parents' means would be taken into account if they asked for financial help with the costs of travel to their child's school. Many social workers said that, as parents retain the mobility allowance of their child's disability living allowance, they would expect them to use that to get to and from school. A team leader said:

Mostly we'd be saying it was the family's responsibility unless there were particular circumstances. I guess it's something we'd look at if they weren't able to access the mobility allowance.

Parents' experience of what happened to relevant social security benefits when their child went to residential school varied and many felt unsure and unsupported in working out what they were entitled to. Some parents had retained the mobility component of their child's disability living allowance and others had not. Most parents of children on 52-week placements had surrendered their child benefit book, but one wrote to the Benefits Agency telling them how much she spent on travelling to see her son and on clothes for him, and her child benefit book was returned.

Patrick's mother was confronted with a range of practical issues at a time when she felt least able to cope with them. She was unsure if she would still be entitled to child benefit or to working families tax credit and needed help in sorting out her entitlements. Another parent spoke of the financial hardship that followed withdrawal of invalid care allowance and disability living allowance when her daughter went away to school:

I've tried to go out to work but there were meetings to go to, there were crisis times and I don't get any money for her whatsoever but she still wants her treats.

Reviews

Parents had varying experiences of the reviews carried out by social workers. Some found them helpful, others worrying. Very few parents were clear what social services' responsibilities were concerning reviews and some did not even know when or whether social workers visited their child at school. A number of parents worried that social workers were looking for reasons to terminate the placement. As one said:

> I think she really doesn't approve of the school and is looking for any excuse … so, even if I have any concerns, I don't like to raise them, not in the review meeting anyway.

What often bothered parents most about reviews was professionals coming who knew their child a little or not at all. Jane's mother said that at her last review a social worker they didn't know came and said that Jane, then nearly 18, needed to be passed to an adult team: 'and that was the end of that. She didn't know anything about Jane, didn't have a clue. They just sent a token gesture.'

Keyworkers similarly had varying experiences of reviews. Luke's keyworker said that she found social services reviews, in contrast to annual reviews of his Statement, very useful, even though she thought they were 'terrifying'. 'Everybody in that room is there for Luke, I'm there to speak for him, his mum's there to speak for him, his social worker's there.' In contrast, Adrian's keyworker complained that his social worker has 'never spent more than ten minutes with Adrian' and yet: 'He tells me things about Adrian rather than asks me about him.'

Officers from the four case study areas told us that, when a child was joint funded, they tried to tie up the education and the social services review on the same day. However, some social workers said they felt that the education review dominated with their own review and issues about care and welfare being 'tagged on' at the end: 'You find that two hours in, just as you're getting to the social services bit, everyone's tired and desperate to leave.' This is particularly unfortunate if social services are not carrying out six-monthly reviews as required by the Children Act regulations for 'looked after' children.

One social worker told us that the 'looked after children' (LAC) procedures were a very helpful tool in dealing with schools. It enabled the social worker to say that she was carrying out statutory duties with which the schools had to co-operate:

> It's one of the times that the LAC stuff is helpful because you can say 'I have to have this' and 'I have to do that' by law. If you went in and said 'I'd quite like this' or 'would you mind', you would get nowhere.

Social workers spoke of their difficulties in including disabled children and young people in reviews. Constraints on time and inexperience around communication issues meant they recognised their failure to 'ascertain a child's wishes and feelings' as required under the Children Act. In one authority a 'communications group' had been established with the support of a research social worker. The group shared knowledge of different communication systems and of personal experiences of good practice. However, there was a general acknowledgement across the four case study areas of the poor practice that had gone on in the past and that still continued: 'It's not good enough to say that the child's views and feelings are represented by the parents … but it's been accepted for many years', said one social worker.

Transition planning and reviews

A transition plan has to be drawn up at the annual review of a child's Statement in Year 9. It must then be reviewed each year and should enable a smooth transition at the ages of 16 and 19. Education authorities must also notify the social services authority about any child who has a Statement at the age of 14 and social services must determine whether s/he will be entitled to assessment and services as a disabled adult. The intention of the legislation and guidance is that all the relevant agencies should work closely together to draw up a transition plan and arrange for its implementation.

Some education officers were clear that their authority was not carrying out its statutory duties in this area. 'We've never had the manpower to do 14+ transition reviews', said one senior manager. 'They were one of those things that we judged weren't life threatening if they didn't happen … so we don't do them … I think we probably get as far as giving [social services] a list of children who are of that age group for a transition review but I don't think we do our statutory duty *re* transition reviews.' The manager of one education department's Deaf Services Team said:

> Their Statement ceases to exist at 16 and I don't know what happens to them, I've no idea. Once they reach 16 I don't know whether they even have reviews.

Social services departments were sometimes unclear about their statutory responsibilities concerning transition. It is easy to see how young people at residential schools who are solely funded by their education authority do not receive the assistance they are entitled to from social services in their transition to adulthood. This is illustrated by the following exchange:

> Social work team manager: I used to get a list from education and I was being asked for my opinion whether under, and I've forgotten what part of the Act it was, whether they could be categorised as being disabled and I would do yes or no or whatever and then send it back … But I haven't seen a list like that for some time.

Interviewer:	What information are you using to decide whether the child is disabled or not?
Social work team manager:	Well, basically, are we aware of the child, has the child ever been known to any member of this team or any other team?
Interviewer:	So what if nobody knows anything about them? [There was a long pause.]
Social work team manager:	And we're assuming they've got a disability?
Interviewer:	Well if you don't know but you're being asked about them?
Social work team manager:	Well I would write back to education saying we are unaware of this child, we have no information about this child whatsoever, cannot give an opinion. And that's where it would end.

In another area, a team manager said: 'The ones I don't know about I will file under miscellaneous', and another manager said:

If they're not known to us we will send a letter to parents saying we've had this request to assess their needs, but we very seldom get them coming back to us.

Nick was nearly 17, and his mother said that social services kept telling her that she would be appointed a transitions worker but that she had not met him yet. Robert's mother knew that he was supposed to have a 14+ review of his Statement but, she said, 'It never happened. We would go to Robert's review and either there would be nobody from education or there would be nobody from social services ... There was always someone missing.' Robert's mother found this particularly galling because she had been told about the social services authority's new 'integrated assessment'.

When a child at residential school did have an allocated social worker, most said they found 14 too young an age to start thinking about future options and that transition planning was difficult because of lack of communication with adult services. 'Transition planning is a nightmare. Often they stay till 19 and 14 is far too young.' One authority was more positive about its transition planning and had begun a system where, when a young person reached the age of 16, adult services would become involved and attend meetings as the secondary partner to children's services. At 17, children's and adult services would switch roles with adult services being the more proactive but with children's services still involved. Then, at 18, adult services would take over.

Conclusions

The message from parents was generally that they felt unsupported by their education and social services authorities during the time that their child was at a residential school. It is probably significant that, in most cases, a considerable amount of conflict between parents and authorities had been part of the decision-making process leading to a placement. Parents could be left feeling that authorities and professionals were more likely to be hostile than sympathetic and this could lead to a tendency to hold back from raising any problems or additional needs a child might have. As Roy's mother said:

Parents hold back from what you want or what the child needs because you fear you'll lose the placement if you become too pushy.

Perhaps the most striking finding, however, was the considerable confusion, and variations in practice, amongst social services professionals about their statutory obligations under the Children Act to children at residential schools. While legal opinion apparently differs on what these obligations are, it is nonetheless clear that practice was generally not very effective in promoting or protecting the children's welfare. In particular, there was sparse contact between social services professionals and children at residential school, little evidence of their 'wishes and feelings' about the placement being ascertained, and apparently few examples of families being helped to maintain their relationships with their children once a placement has been made.

7 Conclusion

Parents interviewed for this study considered a residential placement for their child when their local authority did not provide adequate support in local schools or to families at home. They usually had little information about the decision-making process, and experienced long delays. Following placement, they received little help to maintain their relationship with their child or to monitor the care and education received. Although boarding school was an option most considered reluctantly, almost all the parents believed that the decision was in the best interests of their child given the local alternatives.

Some children and young people described having opportunities that they had not experienced before – having friends being one of the most important things. However, most also told us that they would rather be living at home. Alongside that were their accounts of isolation and failure to meet their needs at previous local schools.

Eighteen out of the children of the 35 parents taking part in our study had gone away before the age of 11 (another six at the age of 11). While it is unusual, it is still the case that some authorities have, within the last three years, placed four and five year olds in residential schools.

Amongst the local authorities, ideological objections to residential education, and concerns about its cost, were important factors in decision making. Panel meetings usually had little opportunity to consider the needs of individual children. There were often disagreements between education and social services, inadequate information about children's needs and circumstances, and not enough time for a full discussion. Decisions could be delayed for many months.

Placements funded solely by the education authority received little monitoring of care standards and children's welfare. Social services departments followed a variety of practices, but very few children received the full protection of the Children Act. Both education and social services professionals admitted that they would rarely know if children were safe and happy, given the difficulties that they had in spending any time with disabled children and young people at boarding school.

We found considerable confusion amongst the sample of 21 authorities in the first stage of this research about their statutory duties towards children at residential schools, a finding confirmed by this more detailed look at four local authorities. In the argument about whether children at residential school have 'looked after' status, it is easy to treat the statutory responsibilities as ends in themselves, rather than as a means to this end. Disabled children at residential schools have human rights to 'active participation in the community', to services which help them to remain part of their families, to their placement being reviewed at regular intervals to ensure that it meets all aspects of their needs, and to be involved in decisions about their care.[1] The status of 'accommodated' and 'looked after' – and the requirements on local authorities under the Children Act – are a means of achieving these ends.

1   UN Convention on the Rights of the Child.

Our research has demonstrated that, in practice, the current legislative framework is not adequately protecting and promoting the interests of disabled children at boarding schools. Clearly, action is required to address this situation, which should start by asking parents and children themselves how local authorities, corporately, can better protect and promote the human rights of disabled children currently placed at residential schools. Local authorities have a corporate duty to promote and protect the human rights of all children in their area and, if they are using public money to pay for a residential school placement, it is particularly necessary that they ensure this placement promotes and protects the child's welfare. Such action is particularly necessary because it is not always clear that local authorities know that much about the boarding schools where children are placed or whether the needs of individual children are being met.

Questions for local authorities

We set out below some questions which we hope will help to focus attention on the needs of disabled children. These questions are addressed to both education and social services departments. Although it would have been possible to separate them out according to each department's functions and responsibilities, we believe that local authorities should take a corporate responsibility for the welfare of disabled children who are placed at residential schools.

- Are you placing children below the age of 11 at boarding school? If so, what are the circumstances leading to these placements and how could they be avoided?

- What do residential schools offer that your local schools do not?

- What do residential schools offer that your local social support and/or health services do not?

- Do learning and social support services recognise the needs of disabled children to have and make friends, and tackle the barriers to this?

- What is your authority doing to increase the availability of local educational and social support options for the groups of children most at risk of being placed out of authority?

- When you make decisions about placements are you looking at the needs of the individual child? What information does the panel have about the child? Have all panel members sufficient time to read all of the relevant paperwork for a panel meeting? Is there anyone in the room who knows the child? What do you know about the proposed placement and how it may meet the child's educational, care, cultural and emotional needs?

- Are the views of disabled children and young people routinely sought and discussed at panel meetings?

- Does the local Continuing Care policy include children and are there clear policies and procedures for joint working and joint funding with local health services?

- What information do you give to parents about the decision-making process? How do you minimise delays in decision making? What support do you give parents in assessing whether a particular placement may meet their child's needs?

- How do you minimise conflict between the authority and parents, and between different parts of the authority?

- How are placements monitored in terms of whether they are meeting a child's educational, care, cultural and emotional needs? Is someone from the authority checking, on at least a six-monthly basis, whether the placement meets the child's educational, emotional, cultural and care needs? Do you recognise that such monitoring is necessary, regardless of whether the child comes under the Children Act regulations for 'looked after' children?

- How much time do educational psychologists and social workers spend with a child when doing a review of the placement? What steps are taken to involve children and young people in the process of reviews (recognising that inviting them to review meetings may not be the best way of doing this)? Are staff given sufficient training to enable them to use a range of communication methods and techniques with disabled children and young people?

- What support do you give to parents to keep in contact with their child? What support do you provide to enable the child to come home as much as possible (including support to the parent when the child is at home)?

- Are parents given information about how they can get advice on social security benefits and work options once their child has gone to residential school?

- What information do you give to parents about how you will assist them to safeguard their child's welfare? What information do you give to them about what to do if they are unhappy with the care or education their child receives at a residential school? If there are concerns about a particular school, are these routinely communicated to parents?

Recommendations for government

We conclude with some recommendations that seek to link some of the findings of our research with some current policy developments.

Quality Protects

One of the objectives in the first round of the Quality Protects initiative was 'arriving at a complete picture of the number and circumstances of disabled children'. However, information relating to disabled children at residential schools has not so far been forthcoming from either the Quality Protects Management Action Plans (Council for Disabled Children, 1999, 2000), or the Children in Need census. Neither is there a national picture of numbers of disabled children at residential schools available from statistics gathered by the Department for Education and Skills. As Sir William Utting pointed out:

It is hard to see how services for disabled children and young people can be managed in a strategic way in the absence of statistics that enable planners at national or local levels to take an overview of what is being provided and for whom. (Utting, 1997, p. 85).

The Department of Health, through the Quality Protects initiative, should require both education and social services authorities to provide information about the numbers and needs of disabled children placed at residential schools.

There is confusion at all levels – the Department of Health, social services authorities and amongst lawyers – about whether disabled children placed at residential school should be accorded the protection of Children Act regulations. However, even if those placements funded by social services departments *do* come under the 'looked after' children procedures, the majority of residential school placements (nationally) are funded solely by education authorities and therefore do not. Our research found that the parents of disabled children placed in boarding school were not supported to maintain contact with their children and that they are rarely supported by anyone from their local authority to monitor the care their child receives.

The Department of Health and the Department for Education and Skills should, through the Quality Protects initiative, encourage local education and social services authorities to jointly take responsibility for protecting and promoting the welfare of disabled children placed at residential schools and for supporting parents in maintaining contact with their children. Monitoring of whether the placement is meeting a child's educational, care, cultural and emotional needs should take place at six-monthly intervals and should involve someone from the placing authority spending time with the child.

There are a number of barriers in the way of educational psychologists (EPs) being involved in annual reviews and monitoring of Statements after a residential placement has been made. These barriers include: the distance between the school and the home authority, the competing demands on educational psychologists' time, and the fact that EPs do not generally hold 'cases' in the way social workers do. The Department for Education and Employment's Working Party on Educational Psychology Services recommended that local education authorities (LEAs) should establish a formal structure for joint working with health and social services, and that educational psychology services should play a key role to ensure there are closer links between education and care plans. In addition, the Working Party recommended that LEAs 'should explore with health and social services opportunities for jointly funded posts' (Department for Education and Employment, 2000, p. 38).

The Department of Health and the Department for Education and Skills should, through the Quality Protects programme, encourage LEAs to support educational psychologists to be closely involved with individual children placed out of authority, and to develop structures and resources for close working relationships between educational psychologists and relevant health and social services professionals.

SEN Action Programme and SEN Code of Practice

One of the Special Educational Needs Co-ordination Projects (established as part of the Action Plan to implement the Department for Education and Employment's *Meeting Special Educational Needs: A Programme for Action*) has focused on the use of out-of-authority provision in the East of England. The ten authorities involved in the Project highlighted many of the same concerns raised by our own research and resolved that, when residential placements are made, 'rigorous systems are in place to monitor the quality of provision, value for money and child protection procedures' (Special Educational Needs Regional Partnerships, 2001). The steps taken to ensure this include: the development of a regional database of all children with a Statement of SEN who are educated in the independent or non-maintained sector, and the establishment of procedures for monitoring such placements. The latter includes assigning each school a 'link LEA' so that knowledge and experience of the school can be built up and then shared with those making placement decisions (see also Castle, 2001).

The Department for Education and Skills should encourage all the SEN Regional Partnerships to establish systems to record out-of-authority placements of children with a Statement of SEN, and to assign each school a Link LEA or similar system to monitor the standard of education and care provided and disseminate information to other LEAs.

One of the main messages from our research is how difficult parents found the current decision-making processes concerning residential school placements. Most parents had little information about how the process worked or who was involved, and they commonly experienced considerable delay and uncertainty about what was happening concerning their child's education. Those education and social services workers in direct contact with parents also found the decision-making process frustrating and unsatisfactory. The revised Code of Practice encourages 'positive attitudes to parents' and 'user-friendly information and procedures', both of which were sadly lacking in the authorities we studied.

The Department for Education and Skills, possibly through the SEN Programme for Action, should encourage the development of good practice in the decision-making processes concerning out-of-authority placements. The Office for Standards in Education (Ofsted) should monitor parental satisfaction with the decision-making process.

The revised Code of Practice states that, when a child attends a residential school, 'every effort should be made to ensure that parents are encouraged to continue to play an active role in their children's education'. The Code also points out that 'the role of an independent parental supporter may be particularly helpful in accompanying parents to meetings or reviews and ensuring they feel able to contribute.' There was no evidence from our research that education authorities currently take such a positive attitude towards encouraging parental involvement when a child is placed at a residential school.

Ofsted should monitor the extent to which LEAs encourage parents to be involved in their child's education following a residential placement and also the provision of independent parental supporters in such situations.

Connexions

Our research confirms earlier findings that the transitional arrangements for young people placed out of their local area are not working well (Social Services Inspectorate, 1995, 1997; Morris, 1999). The new Connexions services is intended to include young disabled people placed at boarding schools within their remit but the responsibility will be shared between the Connexions Partnership in their home area and the partnership where they are based in term time (Connexions, 2001a, p. 17). It is uncertain how this will work and how the Connexions service will link in with existing responsibilities for supporting young disabled people in their transition to adulthood. The Supplementary Guidance issued by Connexions concerning young people with 'learning difficulties or disabilities' makes no mention of young people placed outside their local area (Connexions, 2001b).

A pilot project should be set up to deliver the Connexions service to young disabled people in residential schools. Such a project should establish good practice and disseminate this to all Connexions Partnerships.

Bibliography

Abbott, D., Morris, J. and Ward, L. (2000) *Disabled Children and Residential Schools: A Study of Local Authority Policy and Practice.* Norah Fry Research Centre

Borland, M. *et al.* (1998) *Education and Care away from Home: A Review of Research, Policy and Practice.* Scottish Council for Research in Education

Castle, K. (2001) *Away from Home – the Price Paid: Children with Emotional and Behavioural Difficulties Who Go to Residential School.* London Region SEN Regional Partnership

Chaplain, R. and Freeman, A. (1994) *Caring under Pressure.* David Fulton

Connexions (2001a) *Connexions Service Funding: A Consultation Paper – January 2001.* Department for Education and Employment

Connexions (2001b) *Learning Difficulties and Disabilities: Supplementary Guidance.* Department for Education and Employment

Cooper, P.W. (1992) 'Exploring pupils' perceptions of the effects of residential schooling on children with emotional and behavioural problems', *Therapeutic Care and Education*, Vol. 1, No. 1, pp. 22–34

Council for Disabled Children (1999) *Quality Protects: First Analysis of Management Action Plans with Reference to Disabled Children and Families.* Council for Disabled Children

Council for Disabled Children (2000) *Quality Protects: Second Analysis of Management Action Plans with Reference to Disabled Children and Families.* Council for Disabled Children

Department for Education and Employment (2000) *Educational Psychology Services (England): Current Role, Good Practice and Future Directions, Report of the Working Group.* Department for Education and Employment

Department for Education and Skills (2001) *SEN Code of Practice on the Identification and Assessment of Pupils with Special Educational Needs.* Department for Education and Skills

Dyson, Alan *et al.* (1998) *Effective Communication between Schools, LEAs and Health and Social Services in the Field of Special Educational Needs.* Department for Education and Employment

Gleeson, J. (1999) 'The residential school for special needs: selection and referral process and the therapeutic milieu', *Child Care in Practice*, Vol. 5, No. 1, pp. 45–54

Grimshaw, R. and Berridge, D. (1994) *Education of Disruptive Children: Placement and Progress in Residential Special Schools for Pupils with Emotional and Behavioural Difficulties.* National Children's Bureau

Morgan, R. (1993) *School Life: Pupils' Views on Boarding.* Department of Health

Morris, J. (1998) *Still Missing? Disabled Children and the Children Act.* The Who Cares? Trust

Morris, J. (1999) *Hurtling into a Void: Transition to Adulthood for Young Disabled People with 'Complex Health and Support Needs'.* Pavilion Publishing

Robertson, J. *et al.* (1995) *Where Are They Now? A Follow-up of Children who Have Attended Beech Tree School.* Hester Adrian Research Centre, University of Manchester.

Robertson, J. *et al.* (1996) 'Residential special education for children with severely challenging behaviours: the views of parents', *British Journal of Special Education*, Vol. 23, No. 2, pp. 80–8

Social Services Inspectorate (1995) *Growing Up and Moving On: Report of an SSI Project on Transition Services for Disabled Young People.* Department of Health

Social Services Inspectorate (1997) *Moving On Towards Independence: Second Report of an SSI Project on Transition Services for Disabled Young People.* Department of Health

Special Educational Needs Regional Partnerships (2001) *Case Study 2: The Use of Out-county and Out-city Provision in the East of England.* Department for Education and Employment

Utting, W. (1997) *People Like Us: The Review of the Safeguards of Children Living away from Home.* Department of Health and the Welsh Office

Wilson, C. and Jade, R. (1999) *Whose Voice is it Anyway? Talking to Disabled Young People at School.* Alliance for Inclusive Education

Appendix: Methodology

Getting advice

The project was supported by a reference group of young disabled people who had been, or were, at residential school. They helped particularly with the design of interview schedules for parents and for children and young people. They had suggestions about the best way to carry out interviews and advised on getting key messages from the research to disabled children and young people.

We also had a project advisory group made up of professionals and parents who commented on our methodology, interview schedule design and draft of this report.

'Disabled children'

We took as our definition of 'disabled child' any child whose primary special educational need related to functional (including intellectual) impairment. This meant excluding those children whose primary special educational need was identified as 'emotional and behavioural difficulties'.

The sample of authorities

The first stage of the research gathered information from 21 authorities. At the outset of the research, it had been proposed that a postal survey of local authorities in England would be used to collect data about residential school placements for disabled children. We consulted our advisory group on drafts of this survey but on their advice rejected this approach. Their concerns were that the response rate would be low and that different authorities use different definitions of 'disabled child' or 'residential school placement'. Instead, we visited a sample of 21 authorities and met with senior managers in education and social services who had primary responsibility for making decisions about placing disabled children and young people at residential schools. We collected quantitative data from them about the placements and also carried out a qualitative interview to get their views on why placements were made, the decision-making process, the legislative framework relevant to these children, and co-operation between social services, education and health.

We used a number of criteria in order to draw a representative sample of 21 authorities in the first stage of the research. These were:

- type of authority

- region

- the percentage of pupils with Statements of special educational need

- the percentage of pupils in special schools

- the percentage of secondary school age pupils who were white

- weeks taken to prepare a Statement of SEN (one of the criteria used by the Audit Commission to measure performance of LEAs)

- specialist social work teams: a telephone survey of one in two of English social services departments found that only 10 per cent include disabled children within disability teams catering for adults and children. Ninety per cent of social services departments now have either a specialist social work team for disabled children or specialist workers within generic area social work teams. We ensured our sample reflected this.

For the second stage of the research, we chose four case study local authorities, from the original sample of 21, to look in much closer detail at the decision-making processes and the experiences of families and disabled children at residential school.

We selected these four by using the following criteria:

- type of authority

- region

- children at residential schools as a percentage of pupils with Statements of special educational need: we chose four authorities to include ones with low, average and above-average percentages

- the proportion of appeals of Statements of special educational needs: we chose authorities which had low, average and above-average proportion of appeals

- children from minority ethnic groups: we chose authorities with low, average and above-average percentages of secondary school pupils who were black or Asian

- joint funding of placements: we chose a range of levels of joint funding of placements, using data from the first stage of the research

- specialist social work teams: we chose three areas who have specialist disabled children's teams and one area where responsibility for disabled children is held within disability teams covering both adults and children

- pooled budgets: we also chose one area where education and social services have a pooled budget for out-of-authority placements.

The four areas selected can therefore be described as follows:

- Authority 1: city council, South West England; area-based disabled children social work teams.

- Authority 2: county council, North West England; area-based disabled children social work teams.

- Authority 3: London borough; social services Learning Disability Team and Physical and Sensory Impairment Team have responsibility for disabled children and adults.

- Authority 4: county council, South East England; area-based disabled children social work teams.

Decisions about residential school placements were made in each of the four areas by placement panels. This is how the four panels were constituted:

- Authority 1: decisions about out-of-authority placements made at monthly meetings of a tripartite panel where health, social services and education represented. Panels chaired by education.

- Authority 2: decisions about out-of-authority placements made at monthly meetings of a tripartite panel where health, social services and education represented. Also attended by senior teachers and heads of local residential schools. Panel chaired by education.

- Authority 3: decisions about out-of-authority placements made at monthly panel meetings where social services and education represented. Panel meetings chaired by education and there was a pooled budget.

- Authority 4: decisions about out-of-authority placements made at monthly meetings of a tripartite panel where health, social services and education represented. Panel chaired by education.

We attended panel meetings as observers for a number of months in each authority. We also interviewed a range of key professionals, including social workers and team managers, educational psychologists, staff from hearing and sensory impairment teams, parent partnership workers, SEN assessment officers and managers, and those responsible for out-of-authority placement budgets. In total, we interviewed 53 education and social services professionals.

Talking to parents

We asked each authority to send letters to families involved in the last ten residential school placements made, to include the last five placements funded solely by education and the last five joint funded with social services. The letters invited parents to send back a reply slip to the research team if they were willing to be interviewed. We had an initial 70 per cent response rate (that is, 28 out of 40 parents agreed to be interviewed) and reminder letters elicited two more, meaning that we achieved a 75 per cent response from those parents whose children had most recently been placed at residential schools. We had aimed to interview 40 families and further mailings to parents where placements were not so recent resulted in another four interviews. As a result of this, we interviewed 34 parents. We gave each parent we met a £15 gift voucher as a small token of thanks.

Meeting children and young people

At the end of each interview, we asked parents for their permission to make contact with their child. One parent (whose child had been at residential school for only one week) felt it would not be appropriate for us to meet her child. We therefore wrote directly to 33 children and young people at their schools. We also wrote to one young person, who was the subject of care proceedings, with the permission of her social worker. We wrote to the head teacher and/or head of care telling them about the research, asking them to help the particular child or young person access our letter, if necessary. We received a total of 32 reply slips indicating the young person was willing to be involved. Seven of these responses seemed to be direct from the child or young person, the remainder had either been completed by a support worker or appeared to have been completed with the assistance of a support worker.

We went to schools across all of England. We carried out semi-structured interviews with 18 children and young people, some of whom had communication impairments. We asked for information about communication needs from parents and support workers before visiting the children. We encouraged children and young people to decide for themselves if they wanted another adult to be present during the interview. Eight chose their keyworkers to be there, usually because they wanted them to facilitate communication (one of these needed a sign language interpreter), and ten we met alone.

The remainder of the sample of children and young people (14) had a level of learning difficulty that meant a semi-structured interview was an inappropriate method for gathering information about their views and experiences. Instead, we talked to a keyworker and/or teacher and also spent some time with the young person. We generally spent a whole day at the school, taking part in meals and spending time in the classroom and home part of the school. This allowed interviewers to incorporate their own observations about the children's experiences. We recognise that this still remains 'second-hand' information. However, we did not want to exclude from the research children who could not participate in a 'traditional' interview.

We gave each child and young person a £15 gift voucher of their choice as a small token of our thanks.

Information about the children and young people

Table A1 concerns the children of the 34 parents who participated in the study plus the one young person who was the subject of a care order and who was included in the group of children interviewed.

Table A1 Information about the disabled children and young people in the research (35 in total)

	Number of children	Percentage of the interview sample	Percentage from the 21 authorities involved in stage 1 of the research
Gender			
Male	22	63	69
Female	13	37	31
Current age			
11 or below	8	23	13[a]
12–15	18	51	
16+	9	26	
Age originally went to boarding school			
11 or below	24	69	
12–15	8	23	
16+	3	9	
Ethnic origin			
White	28	80	
Asian	3	9	
African/Caribbean	3	9	
Mixed background	1	3	
Impairment[b]			
Autistic spectrum disorder	11	31	17
Learning disability	10	29	37
Physical disability	8	23	14
Deaf or hearing impaired	4	11	13
Visual impairment	1	3	6
Specific learning difficulty	1	3	7

[a] *We asked the 21 authorities in the first stage of the research how many disabled children currently at boarding school were of primary school age. So, we only know how many children were aged 11 or under.*

[b] *In addition to the figures given here, the breakdown of primary special educational needs (SEN) in the figures returned by the 21 local authorities in the first stage of the research included 6 per cent of children under a category 'other'.*

There are some differences in the profile of children in the second stage of the research in comparision with the total number of children at residential school across the 21 authorities in the first stage of the study. Amongst this current sample, there are a higher proportion of children with a diagnosis of autism (31 per cent compared to 17 per cent in the first stage); a higher proportion of children whose primary SEN is physical disability (23 per cent compared to 14 per cent) and a lower proportion of children with a learning disability (29 per cent compared to 37 per cent). Reasons for these variations may include the following:

- Information on primary SEN in the first stage came from the local education authorities, while, in the second stage, we asked parents what their child's primary SEN was. This may account for some of the variation.

- The data relating to children placed at residential schools in the 21 authorities participating in the first stage of the research concerned the current number of disabled children in placements made stretching back over many years. In contrast, stage 2 focused on the most recent placements. There is anecdotal evidence, and this study would seem to bear this out, that children with autistic spectrum disorder account for an increasing number of residential school placements.

- The variations in the percentages of children with a physical disability and those with a learning disability may be at least partly accounted for by the way information about primary SEN was recorded. It is likely that, in the past, some children with autistic spectrum disorder were included in the category 'learning disability': more accurate diagnosis and greater recognition of autistic spectrum disorder by education professionals has accounted for some, though not all, of the increase in the number of children with autistic spectrum disorder nationally.

- The breakdown of primary SEN in the figures returned by the 21 local authorities in the first stage of the research included a category 'other' and it may be that some children with multiple impairments were included in that category, while in our sample they were included under 'physical disability'.

However, whatever the reasons for the variations in the breakdown of primary SEN between the first stage and the second stage, we are confident that the children included in this second stage are representative of recently made placements as we had such a high response rate from parents and children.